Practical Azure Application Development

A Step-by-Step Approach to Build Feature-Rich Cloud-Ready Solutions

Thurupathan Vijayakumar

Apress®

Practical Azure Application Development

Thurupathan Vijayakumar
Colombo, Sri Lanka

ISBN-13 (pbk): 978-1-4842-2816-6   ISBN-13 (electronic): 978-1-4842-2817-3
DOI 10.1007/978-1-4842-2817-3

Library of Congress Control Number: 2017943372

Cover image designed by Freepik

Managing Director: Welmoed Spahr
Editorial Director: Todd Green
Acquisitions Editor: Nikhil Karkal
Development Editor: Laura Berendson
Technical Reviewer: Pranab Majumdar
Coordinating Editor: Prachi Mehta
Copy Editor: Karen Jameson
Compositor: SPi Global
Indexer: SPi Global
Artist: SPi Global

Distributed to the book trade worldwide by Springer Science+Business Media New York, 233 Spring Street, 6th Floor, New York, NY 10013. Phone 1-800-SPRINGER, fax (201) 348-4505, e-mail orders-ny@springer-sbm.com, or visit www.springeronline.com. Apress Media, LLC is a California LLC and the sole member (owner) is Springer Science + Business Media Finance Inc (SSBM Finance Inc). SSBM Finance Inc is a **Delaware** corporation.

For information on translations, please e-mail rights@apress.com, or visit http://www.apress.com/rights-permissions.

Apress titles may be purchased in bulk for academic, corporate, or promotional use. eBook versions and licenses are also available for most titles. For more information, reference our Print and eBook Bulk Sales web page at http://www.apress.com/bulk-sales.

Any source code or other supplementary material referenced by the author in this book is available to readers on GitHub via the book's product page, located at www.apress.com/978-1-4842-2816-6. For more detailed information, please visit http://www.apress.com/source-code.

Printed on acid-free paper

This book is dedicated to my loving parents

Contents at a Glance

Contents

About the Author

Thurupathan Vijayakumar (Thuru) is an associate solutions architect at Tiqri (www.tiqri.com) and a Microsoft Azure MVP. Thuru has been involved in the design and development of various software solutions for many enterprises and startups. Thuru is a versatile speaker and a known blogger. He specializes in software design, business intelligence, the security development life cycle, and data intelligence services. He lives in Colombo and enjoys traveling and eating. Blog: www.thuru.net, Twitter: @thurutweets.

About the Technical Reviewer

Pranab Majumdar is currently working as an Escalation Engineer for the Microsoft Azure SQL Database and Azure SQL Datawarehouse. He will be moving as an Embedded Escalation Engineer working very closely and partnering with the Engineering team. Prior to getting aligned to the Cloud side of the Business, he was an Escalation Engineer with the SQL Server team in CSS/GBS where he worked with the Product Team to fix bugs within the SQL Server Product thereby making SQL a better and Preferred RDBMS. He has been working with Microsoft for close to 12 years now with his specialization in SQL Server Engine, Performance, High Availability and disaster recovery. He has worked with a lot of large corporates with huge and very large and complex SQL deployments..

Apart from SQL he has also been working with operational Insight formerly known as System Centre Advisor, migrating and helping create new set of rules and validation process. He holds a number of Microsoft certifications like MCAD, MCSD, MCDBA, MSCE, MCTS, MCITP and MCT since 2005. The latest one being Azure certified. He likes to be connected to the customers and he has been a speaker in TechEd, GIDs, SQL Saturday, SQL Talks, and other Community UG Events.

Acknowledgments

Practical Azure Application Development: *A Step-by-Step Approach to Build Feature-Rich Cloud-Ready Solutions* is a knowledge source that explains different Azure services and how to use them in building enterprise-level software solutions.

Most of the content of this book has been acquired from knowledge and experience gathered during my tenure at Tiqri Corp, and I am grateful for the company and my team.

I am thankful to my colleagues who gave support and courage in writing this book and guiding me towards the completion; my special thanks goes to Ms. Thushara Wijewardena, CPO of Tiqri, who motivated me continuously from the beginning to the completion of this book.

I wish to thank Laura Berendson, Nikhil Karkal, and Prachi Mehta from Apress who assisted me in many ways, in completing this book.

Introduction

The terms Cloud computing or Microsoft Azure are not new to the industry. Azure has been one of the leading and well-proven cloud platforms, which creates a growing demand for the Azure skills in the industry.

Although Azure has many knowledge sources, they all lack a fundamental aspect of creating solutions using Azure services. Those knowledge sources target the specific service offering of the Azure and shows what it is and how it works, but in reality we use many different cloud services as a combined package to deliver the solutions.

Practical Azure Application Development: *A Step-by-Step Approach to Build Feature-Rich Cloud-Ready Solutions* – fills the skill gap and targets **how a real-world problem can be modeled on top of different Azure services and how those services can be leveraged in cutting down development effort while considering the right options for the problem in hand.**

This books covers 13 different Azure services that are very common in enterprise application development scenarios, including the basic DevOps cycle. The book begins by detailing how to obtain an Azure account to using different services in different stages of the application development with the help of a sample multitenant-based document management solution. The book has the accompanying code for each chapter that helps the readers to try out what they learn.

This solution-based unique approach makes this book a special guide in Azure application development space and an interesting read.

CHAPTER 1

■ ■ ■

Azure – A Solutions Development Platform

The term "cloud solution" or the amplified declaration of "we are running on cloud" is not new to the modern software developers. Developing solutions for cloud has two aspects. One of them is thinking and architecting the application for the implications of cloud, such as cost, latency, data protection, etc. The second aspect is knowing the tools and services available for a chosen cloud platform and leveraging them to design solutions.

Knowing the tools and services available from a chosen cloud platform and having the understanding of how they work is a definite advantage for the developers in creating efficient and reliable solutions for the specific platform. More often these skills are conceptually transferable to different cloud platforms as well.

In that ground concept, this chapter introduces Microsoft Azure as a solutions development platform for enterprises. Azure has a myriad of services that facilitate a large spectrum of solutions, ranging from legacy business applications to highly scalable solutions powered by the cutting-edge artificial intelligent services and analytics. In order to build effective solutions on Azure, developers should have the right understanding and the knowledge about these services.

Let's Define IaaS, PaaS, and SaaS

Infrastructure as a Service (IaaS), Platforms as a Service (PaaS), and Software as a Service(SaaS) - these are the highly disputed terms in the IT industry. They are not new and often heard, but still the confusion about those **three base cloud service models** remain constant among the developers.

Since this entire book focuses on the Azure platform services and how to use them to build the modern enterprise applications, it is essential to have a demarcation among these service models, at least for the context of this book.

Infrastructure as a Service (IaaS)

This model gives the flexibility and the control **closer to the on-premises topological layout of the computing resources**. The resources are often addressed in terms of virtual machines, load balancers, networking infrastructure, and so on. Users are responsible

© Thurupathan Vijayakumar 2017

T. Vijayakumar, *Practical Azure Application Development*, DOI 10.1007/978-1-4842-2817-3_1

for managing not only the applications but also the data, runtime, middleware, and operating systems of the infrastructure.

Platform as a Service (PaaS)

This model gives the **computing resources as services and APIs to build solutions**. Developers use these cloud service components and build custom applications. Users are free from managing the computing resources, runtime, middleware, and operating systems. They can focus on the business application development and the problem in hand. The Azure PaaS offering is the primary focus of this book.

Software as a Service (SaaS)

This model offers **ready-made software solutions delivered through the Internet** with the cloud characteristics of scalability, high availability, etc. Any software solution that is delivered as a service that can be consumed directly by the end user for the business usage can be categorized into this model.

Note   Though the mentioned three are the three base service models of any cloud platform, you can see many derivatives of these service models in the market. Some of these derivatives include Data as a Service, NoSQL as a Service, Identity as a Service, Desktop as a Service, and many more.

Also, due to the automation and management aspects of the modern cloud platforms, you can see those three service models have some degree of characteristics shared and intersect among themselves as well.

Example – A software as a service application having an API and allowing data storage acts as a platform as a service model. A platform as a service virtual machine environment allows remote connections and custom application configurations and acts as infrastructure as a service as well.

Read more about the PaaS model in Azure from this link. This link also explains how the three service models are aligned in Azure. `https://azure.microsoft.com/en-us/overview/what-is-paas/`

PaaS Services of Azure

Azure has a number of PaaS services; this book covers the most common services used in enterprise application development. Following are some of the PaaS services explained in this book with the help of a simple document management application named DashDocs.

- **Azure Web Apps** – This is one of the app types available under the Azure App Services. This is a web server as a service model and used in hosting web applications. Web applications written on .NET, Java, NodeJs, and PHP can be deployed in Azure Web Apps.

- **Azure SQL Database** – SQL database as a service model. This is the primary and the only relational database as service available in Azure.

- **Azure Blob Storage** – Azure-based object store for storing binary large objects. Also, it serves as the disk storage for the virtual machines.

- **Azure Document DB** – Azure-based document type NoSQL database service. Very handy in developing social applications that demand modern social features with high throughput and flexibility.

- **Redis on Azure** – The known Redis cache on Azure, as a platform service this eases the usage by eliminating the management and maintenance overhead.

- **Azure Table Storage** – Key-attribute type NoSQL database as a service. Highly scalable and capable of handling immense amount of data and throughput. Highly cost-effective solution.

- **Azure Search** – Search as a service on Azure, which has the capability of indexing varieties of data sources and can be scaled to greater demands. Simplifies the search development.

- **Azure Active Directory (AAD)** – Commonly categorized under identity as a service model. A cloud-based identity management service. Can be synced with on-premises Active Directory as well. Facilitates identity management, monitoring, single sign-on, etc.

- **Azure Power BI Embedded** – In simple words, this is Power BI as a service with custom application features. Can be integrated into the custom applications and has rendering-based pricing model.

- **Azure Key Vault** – Key management store as a service, which has the capability of Hardware Security Modules (HSM) and facilitates importing the on-premises key stores to Azure.

- **Azure API Management** – API Management is a platform tool to expose, document, and secure APIs while facilitating developers. This is a comprehensive service in managing all the aspects of APIs of a business.

Azure Account and Subscriptions

In order to start using Azure or develop solutions using Azure services, first we need an account in Azure. An Azure account can be acquired by many ways; there are various options available like trial versions, MSDN subscriptions, BizSpark offers, credit card purchase models, enterprise agreements, and so on.

Leaving those complexities and various options aside, let's discuss the typical purchase model of Azure using the credit card, as it is the common method among individual developers and SMEs. Regardless of the method how you own an Azure account, the experience is very much the same.

Go to `https://azure.microsoft.com/en-us/free/` and sign up for a free Azure account. This book skips the steps of signing up for a new Azure account, since documenting the experience is very volatile and the specified link will guide you on the account creation process.

You would submit an email address during the account creation process at some point; these credentials you used in the sign-up process will become the credentials of the **Azure account administrator; one Azure account can have only one account administrator**.

An Azure account is a collection of Azure subscriptions, and subscriptions are the workspace of Azure. Creating an Azure account means that you're creating your first Azure subscription within the account.

Account administrator automatically becomes the Service administrator of a subscription. The account administrator is the person who is authorized to access **Account Center** (`https://account.windowsazure.com/`); Account Center is used to create and manage subscriptions.

Different subscriptions within an Azure account can have different payment methods. As an example, if one Azure account has two subscriptions then the first subscription would have a pay-as-you-go model and the second one would have the fixed amount limitation for monthly use.

Service administrator can create co-administrators, and co-administrators also can create other co-administrators. One subscription can have more than one co-administrator. Co-administrators have full access to the Azure services in the subscription except the permissions to manage the Azure Active Directory (AAD).

Service administrators and co-administrators are known as Subscription Admins in the new portal. The explicit difference between a service administrator and a co-administrator in the scope of a subscription is that the service administrator has the Global Admin role in AAD and the co-administrator has the User role. So, unless specifically assigned to a Global Admin role, a co-administrator would not have permissions to manage AAD.

Refer to this example to understand the subscription administrators and their access level.

Linda signs up for the Azure account, so she becomes the account administrator and the service administrator of the subscription 1. Later she creates another subscription (subscription 2) under the same Azure account. She adds Tim as a co-administrator to subscriptions 1 and 2. She adds Bob as co-administrator to subscription 2. Figure 1-1 shows the eventual administrator role assignments.

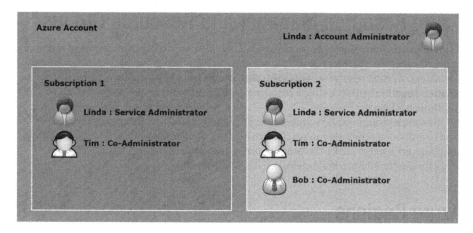

Figure 1-1. *Azure subscriptions and administrator assignments*

Azure service administrator and co-administrator (subscription admins) are Azure-specific roles and not AAD roles. **In the new portal, access to Azure resources can be managed using Role Based Access Control (RBAC).** Users who are not subscription admins can get the permissions to access the new portal and specific resources using RBAC permissions.

■ **Note**   In order to perform all the steps specified in this book, you should at least have the credentials of co-administrator with Global Admin role in the AAD.

Azure Deployment Models

Azure resources are the instances of Azure services, and they are created inside the Azure subscriptions. **Azure has two resource deployment models, classic model and Azure Resource Manager (ARM) model.**

Microsoft says, "The Resource Manager and classic deployment models represent two different ways of deploying and managing your Azure solutions. You work with them through two different API sets, and the deployed resources can contain important differences. The two models are not completely compatible with each other." (https://docs.microsoft.com/en-us/azure/azure-resource-manager/resource-manager-deployment-model)

The main benefit and the reason for ARM to be the successor of the classic model is that **it allows the Azure resources to be managed as groups known as resource groups**.

The classic Azure deployment is getting obsolete; resources created via the Azure classic portal (https://manage.windowsazure.com) often take the classic deployment model.

This book follows the ARM deployment model and uses the new Azure portal (https://portal.azure.com) experience.

Azure Resource Manager and Resource Groups

As mentioned, Azure Resource Manager (ARM) is the new deployment model of Azure. Azure resources are placed inside resource groups. Resource groups act as the grouping containers of Azure resources. **This grouping allows us to keep the resources of a solution together within a single resource group and manage the resources as a solutions package.**

Resource groups can be scripted using ARM templates, and these scripts can be used to automate the deployments and create similar environments. In Chapter 3, ARM templates are used to create the production environment of the application from the template generated from the development resource group.

Azure Regions

Azure is a cloud product that runs on massive Microsoft datacenters. These datacenters are in different geographical regions. Azure is generally available in 30 regions as of the date of this writing. Read more about the Azure regions from this link: `https://azure.microsoft.com/en-us/regions/`

You should select the Azure region for each resource you create, always choosing the region that is closer to your customers or end users. You can also deploy resources in multiple regions to cater to customers from different regions and apply load balancing and traffic routing techniques.

There are occasions that you cannot select the region which is closest to your customers.

1. One such occasion is where some resources are not available in all the regions, so you need to select the region where the resource is available.

2. Organizations have policies to keep their resources within a specific geographic boundary due to some organizational and political concerns, so you need to select the appropriate region to cater to this requirement.

3. In certain special scenarios, organizations opt for special datacenters. Microsoft has few datacenters that cater to such special requirements from governments. You can read more about them from this link: `https://www.microsoft.com/en-us/trustcenter/CloudServices/NationalCloud`

Introduction to Azure Portal

Visit `https://portal.azure.com` and log in with your credentials. You will see the Azure portal dashboard, similar to the screenshot in Figure 1-2.

Figure 1-2. Azure portal dashboard

In the left-hand side, the menu displays the frequently accessed options of the Azure account.

On top of this menu notice the 'New' button. You can create Azure resources by clicking this button, searching for the specified resources and filling the blade with the respective parameters.

Each resource has a different UI template that is specific to that resource. The UI experience of panels spanning horizontally in the screen is quite unique to the new Azure portal; **these panels are known as blades**.

Get familiar with the portal experience, as it is very comprehensive; try navigating through various resource options, pinning items in the dashboard, resizing the tiles, etc.

■ **Note** Azure and Azure resources can be managed through the portal and Azure web portal remains the main visual experience. It is a friendly tool and good to begin with. But Azure can be accessed and managed by various other methods as well; mainly Visual Studio 2015 has a rich Azure management experience, PowerShell is a great tool in managing Azure, and Azure exposes a management REST API as well. Other than these methods, there are various third-party tools available to manage the Azure as a whole or to manage specific Azure services.

Azure Compliances

Azure is complaint with many standards and regulations making it the best fit for many enterprise-level applications. In fact, Azure claims that it has more certifications than any other cloud provider. It has certifications including ISO/IEC, CSA/CCM, HIPPA, ITAR, CJIS IRS 1075, and many more.

You can read more about how Azure operates in terms of security and data governance and various Azure certifications and compliances from `https://azure.microsoft.com/en-us/support/trust-center/`

Introduction to DashDocs Application

DashDocs is a cloud-based document management application. It is the sample used in this book, in order to explore the different services of Azure and explain the practical usage scenarios.

DashDocs is developed using ASP.NET MVC using Visual Studio 2015 with Azure SDK 2.9 on .NET version 4.6. You can get the full source code of the application from this GitHub repository: `https://github.com/thuru/DashDocs`

DashDocs Application

DashDocs is an Azure Active Directory (AAD)-based multitenant document management application. Organizations get registered with DashDocs using their AADs.

Users can upload and download documents. They also can post comments about the documents and view usage reports.

In order to leverage and span the experience across many Azure services, DashDocs uses different services as much as possible. The DashDocs development pipeline is based on the Visual Studio Team Services (VSTS) DevOps practices.

Table 1-1 explains the different Azure services used in DashDocs.

Table 1-1. *Azure services and DashDocs features mapping*

Azure Service	Feature
Azure Web Apps	DashDocs application is hosted in Azure Web Apps
SQL Database	Used to store application data
Blob Storage	Used to store documents
Table Storage	Used in application logging
Application Insights	Monitoring application and telemetry data collection
Azure Active Directory	Enabling multitenancy with single sign-on
Redis Cache	Caching frequently accessed data
Azure Search	Enabling search functionality in the application
Azure Key Vault	Key Management Store for managing encryption keys
Power BI Embedded	Enables reporting and Power BI visualizations
Document DB	User to store comments for the documents

Summary

Azure is a feature-rich proven cloud platform from Microsoft. It offers all three service models of cloud computing and has strong compliancy for enterprise application development.

The rest of the book covers the major platform services of Azure with the help of the DashDocs application and how we can leverage them together in developing enterprise solutions using seven comprehensive chapters.

Chapter 1 – Covers the introduction to cloud computing and Azure services including compliancy, basic usage model, and the introduction to the DashDocs application.

Chapter 2 – Covers Azure Web Apps, SQL Database, and Blob Storage. In this chapter we begin the development of the DashDocs application. Application data will be stored in the SQL Database using Entity Framework code first approach, and documents will be stored in Azure Blob Storage. The DashDocs application itself is a, ASP MVC application.

Chapter 3 – Covers the DevOps aspects of the application. We would create a Git repo in VSTS, create build definitions, and enable continuous integration and deployment to Azure Web App. Azure Application Insights will be used in application monitoring.

Chapter 4 – Covers the integration with the Azure Active Directory (AAD) and enables multitenancy and single sign-on to the application. The chapter covers other identity management aspects like Role Based Access Control (RBAC) as well.

Chapter 5 – This chapter covers the NoSQL services of the Azure. We will store application logs in the Azure table storage, add integration with Redis cache for the recent documents, and will use Document DB for the user comments for the documents.

Chapter 6 – Covers the security services available in Azure, especially the data security features like encryption with Azure Key Vault and other built-in data security aspects.

Chapter 7 – Covers the Azure Search service and integration with the DashDocs application.

Chapter 8 – Covers the data visualization as a service in the Azure. Power BI Embedded is used to visualize the reports of the DashDocs application.

CHAPTER 2

▨ ▨ ▨

Beginning Application Development with Azure Web Apps, SQL Database, and Blob Storage

In this chapter, we will begin the development of the DashDocs application while exploring three very common services of Azure: Azure Web Apps, SQL Database, and Blob Storage. Azure Web Apps is used to host the application, SQL Databases is the relational database as a service used to persist data, and Blob storage is used to store the documents.

In the initial version of the application we should be able to upload/download documents to and from Blob storage, and basic application data are stored in the SQL Database.

Beginning DashDocs Application Development

DashDocs is a cloud-based document management software as a service for enterprises, where organizations can create their own space and manage their documents and users. First create the ASP.NET MVC web application; begin the process by selecting the available ASP.NET MVC web application template in Visual Studio as shown in Figure 2-1.

▨ **Note** Throughout this book DashDocs is used to explain various Azure services, but the implementation of this application is not a guideline or a standard enterprise-level template.

© Thurupathan Vijayakumar 2017
T. Vijayakumar, *Practical Azure Application Development*, DOI 10.1007/978-1-4842-2817-3_2

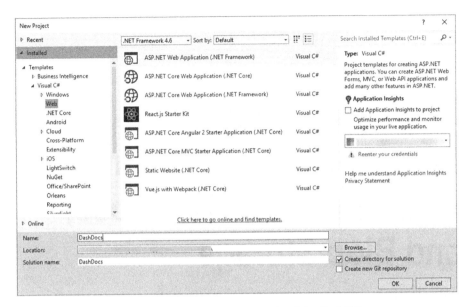

Figure 2-1. *Creating ASP.NET MVC Application in Visual Studio 2015*

Select MVC template and select Web API as an additional core reference (Refer to Figure 2-2). Click on the 'Change Authentication' button and select 'No Authentication' as we do not require authentication at this stage. Chapter 4 describes Azure Active Directory (AAD) authentication in multitenancy mode.

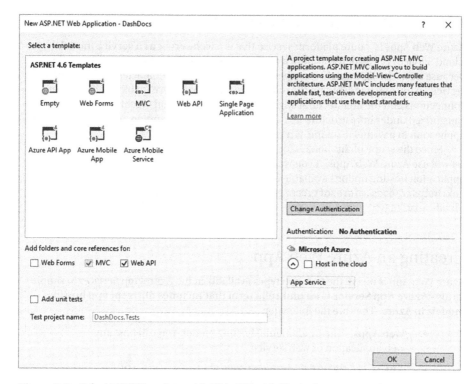

Figure 2-2. *Select MVC Template with Web API with No Authentication option.*

Getting Started with Azure Web Apps

Azure Web Apps is the first Azure service we will work with in the DashDocs application development process. It is a powerful platform to host the web applications and provide greater scalability. It supports different deployment models and runtimes.

Choosing the Hosting Option

Azure Web Apps is a platform service that made the web application development and publication tremendously easy. However, there are several other options available in Azure for hosting web applications - Cloud Services, Virtual Machines, Service Fabric, and more.

Since there is more than one option available to host the web applications and on the surface, all the options have their own justification, developers often find it confusing to choose the right hosting option. **This confusion is quite prominent among the web apps, cloud services, and virtual machines compared to the other options.**

Web Apps vs. Cloud Services vs. VMs

Azure Web Apps is a pure platform service that is a **web server as a service model**. Cloud Service is considered as both a platform service and as an infrastructure service because it has the lightweight management and deployment characteristics of a platform service on the one hand; but on the other hand it also has rich capabilities like remote connections and the architectural alignment with Azure virtual machines, leaving it to be categorized under infrastructure as a service as well. The last option, which is hosting the application in a virtual machine, is a pure infrastructure as service model.

Since the scope of this book is focused primarily on platform services of Azure, we will use Azure Web Apps. If you want to read the comparison between the different application hosting options available in Azure in detail, you can read more from this link: https://docs.microsoft.com/en-us/azure/app-service-web/choose-web-site-cloud-service-vm

Creating an Azure Web App

Azure Web App is one of the four app types available in the Azure App Service. In simple terms - **Azure App Service is an umbrella term that includes different app hosting models in Azure**. They are the following:

- **Web Apps** – The fundamental hosting model. You can host any web application or web service.

- **API Apps** – Web apps equipped with API features like API documentation endpoints, CORS settings, and more.

- **Mobile Apps** – Web apps equipped with features favoring mobile development, like data sync, push notifications, and more.

- **Logic Apps** – Workflows and integration as a service model, includes enterprise integrations and social integration connectors and allows custom connectors to be developed and used as well.

■ **Note**   Though API Apps and Mobile Apps have some specific features for the respective API and mobile usage scenarios, those features can be developed, enabled, and deployed using Web Apps as well. Azure Web Apps remain the foundation of the other app services except logic apps as it has a different design model and functional approach.

Now that we have a raw web application in the Visual Studio created from the template, let's host the application in an Azure Web App. Create a Web App using Azure portal. First, log in to the portal using your credentials and create a resource group named 'DashDocsDev' by simply clicking on the 'New' button and searching for the Resource Groups option. Fill the name (DashDocsDev) and select the location; finally hit 'Create'. Refer to Figure 2-3.

Figure 2-3. *Creating the DashDocsDev Resource Group*

Now let's create a Web App inside the resource group. Click the 'New' button search for Web Apps and select the Web App option from the blade (Figure 2-4). There are other Web App options also available, packaged with different databases, in this case choose the Web App only option.

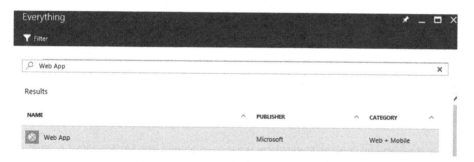

Figure 2-4. *Choosing the Web App*

In the Web App creation blade (Figure 2-5), fill in the details of your web application. Fill in the name of your web app (dashdocs-dev is used in this book), which will generate the URL http://dashdocs-dev.azurewebsites.net) of the Web App.

In the Resource Group option choose 'Use existing' option and select the DashDocsDev Resource Group from the drop-down. By doing this we're putting the Web App in our development Resource Group.

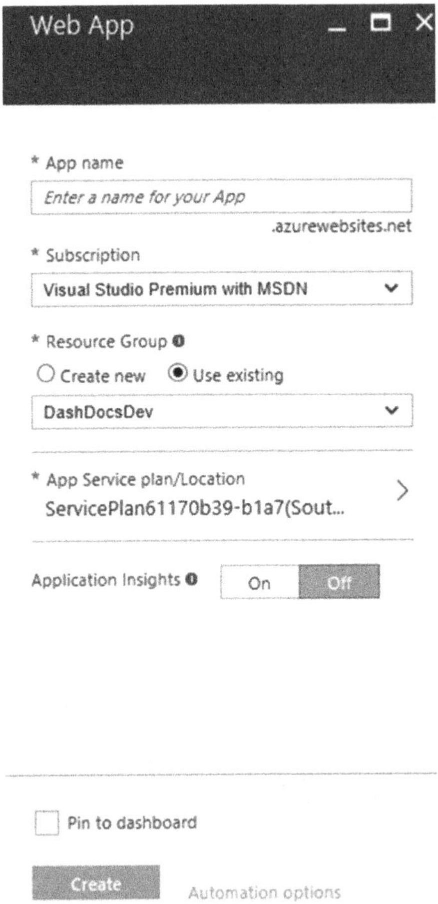

Figure 2-5. Web App creation blade

In the Web App creation blade, there is a section named App Service plan/Location. **App Service Plan decides the grouping of your Azure App Service apps.** Apps packaged under the same App Service Plan have the same region and scalability settings.

Azure App Service Plan

If you have a solution that is a composite of more than one app, **placing them in the same App Service Plan would give the flexibility of scaling them at once** by scaling the App Service Plan, thus eliminating the effort of scaling them individually.

App Service Plans are bound to the locations, creating services in the same App Service Plan make them reside in the same region and eliminating network latencies.

Let's create a custom App Service Plan (DashDocsDevelopmentPlan) in order to manage development apps using a single App Service Plan. Click on the App Service Plan option in the Web App creation blade (Figure 2-5).

This will open up the App Service Plan creation blade (Figure 2-6). Name the App Service Plan, select the location, select the right pricing tier, and create the App Service Plan. After creating the App Service Plan, navigate back to the Web App creation blade and complete the Web App creation process.

Figure 2-6. *App Service Plan creation blade*

■ **Note** You can read more about different Azure App Service Plans from this link: https://azure.microsoft.com/en-us/pricing/details/app-service/plans/. Different Azure App Service Plans provide different resources for the selection and deployment. You can always start with the lower tier and scale up to higher tiers or scale out the number of instances we need to have.

Azure Web Apps Deployment Options

We can host the web application and get the first deployment experience. Though the web application we created from the Visual Studio template has no application-specific features, hosting it in the Azure would give some firsthand practical Azure experience.

There are several methods available to deploy a web application to Azure Web App.

You can perform it directly from Visual Studio – which includes the creation of App Service Plan and Web App from the Visual Studio itself. The second option is explicitly publishing the content from Visual Studio using the publishing profile downloaded from the Web App. The third option would be using the good old FTP method with a preferred FTP client. Fourth, but not the least option, would be creating an automated CI/CD DevOps deployment pipeline.

In order to keep things simple, this chapter explains the third option: explicitly publishing the content from Visual Studio using the publishing profile.

Chapter 3 explains the DevOps process of build automation, deployments, environment management, and monitoring with the integration of Visual Studio Team Services (VSTS) and Azure, which is the common scenario in enterprise application development.

Publishing the Application from Visual Studio

In order to publish the web application content from Visual Studio, we need the publishing profile downloaded from the Web App. Select the Web App in the portal and download the publishing profile (Figure 2-7).

Figure 2-7. *Download the publishing profile.*

Publish setting files are named in the format of *yourwebappname.PublishSettings*, in this case *dashdocs-dev.PublishSettings*.

In Visual Studio, you will get the publish option when you right-click on the web application project. Selecting the Publish option will open the Publish window (Figure 2-8). In the publish window, click on Import and browse the downloaded publish settings file.

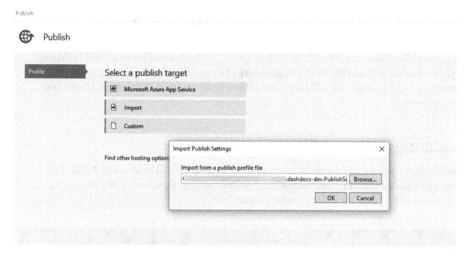

Figure 2-8. *Visual Studio Web App publishing window*

The wizard will guide you through the publishing process; since this is a fresh web application without any custom application/connection settings, simply click through the wizard and finally click on Publish. This will start the deployment. **Visual Studio output window will display the progress of the publish and launch the site once the publish has been completed**. After the publishing process, you should be able to see your web application in the browser using your Web App URL.

Exploring the Publish Settings File

Open the Publish Settings file using a preferred tool (it is a simple XML file). Notice it has two ***publishProfile*** tags inside the ***publishData*** tag.

You will see one publish profile has the details for the MSDeploy publishing option and the second has the details for the FTP option. You can note this with the ***publishMethod*** attribute.

Visual Studio grabs these settings and deploys the application to the Azure Web App. In the explicit publishing method explained in the previous sections, we used the default settings where the publishing method is Web Deploy. In that case, Visual Studio would have used the MSDeploy settings from the publish settings file.

You can use the FTP credentials available in the publish settings file to establish the FTP connection to the Web App.

Getting Started with Azure SQL Database

DashDocs will use SQL Database to store the application data. SQL Database is the relational database as a service offering of Azure. In the development of the DashDocs application we will use the Entity Framework (EF) code-first approach with the SQL Database. At this stage, we will begin with three basic entities: Customers, Users, and Documents.

Creating an Azure SQL Database

Before we begin, we need a database server and a blank SQL Database in Azure. In the Azure portal click the New button and search for SQL Database. Click on the SQL Database option and then click Create (Figure 2-9).

Figure 2-9. *SQL Database selection blade*

In the new SQL Database blade (Figure 2-10), you can enter the name of your database, select the subscription, resource group (DashDocsDev), and blank database as the source.

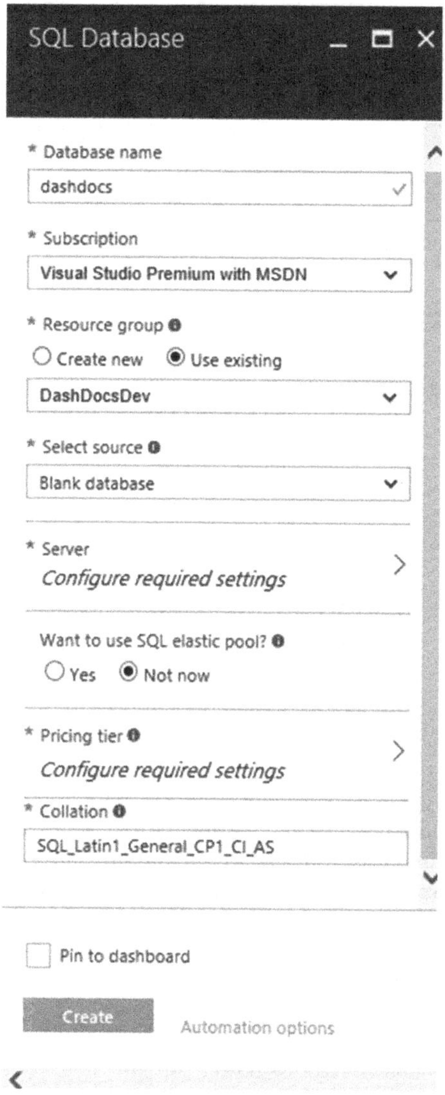

Figure 2-10. SQL Database creation blade

In the server section let's create a new server for the database. **Database servers in Azure SQL Database are logical servers.** Click on the 'Configure required settings' option under the SQL Server section to open the SQL Database Server creation blade (Figure 2-11).

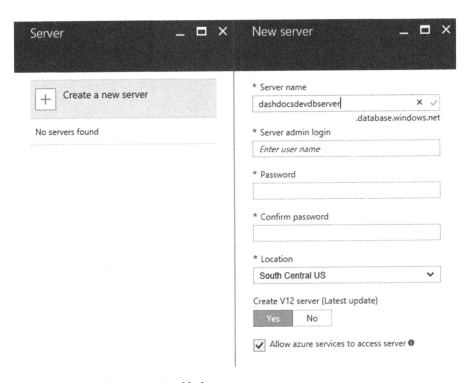

Figure 2-11. SQL Server creation blade

Name your server (dashdocsdevdbserver) and create the admin login to the database server. Leave the V12 setting as it is, since it is the latest version. Leave the 'Allow azure services to access server' ticked; if you untick this, you need to add the correct IP range in firewall settings in order to make the Azure services access your database server. Complete the SQL Server creation process.

Back in the SQL Database blade, notice the question below the Server section – Want to SQL Elastic pool? **You can add the SQL Databases to a pool at a later stage as well**, so leave the option 'Not Now'.

Next option in the blade is selecting the pricing tier for the database. Like other Azure services, SQL Databases also have the pricing options combined with the performance and the scalability aspects of the service.

You can read about different pricing and service options of the Azure SQL Databases from this link: https://docs.microsoft.com/en-us/azure/sql-database/sql-database-service-tiers.

Performance of an SQL Database is measured in a unit known as Data Throughput Unit (DTU). Choose a tier with a lower DTU for the DashDocs application since this is a development database. Read more about DTUs from this link: https://docs.microsoft.com/en-us/azure/sql-database/sql-database-what-is-a-dtu.

■ **Note** SQL Elastic pool helps to create a pool of SQL Databases and manage them from a single execution point; also an SQL Elastic pool manages the load of the databases dynamically by sharing the DTUs among the databases in the pool.

This is a very handy option when managing many databases with the same schema. In a dedicated databases approach where each customer has her dedicated database, there is a high possibility that we end up managing many databases with the same schema.

DashDocs does not use the SQL Elastic pool since it follows the shared databases approach, storing information of all the customers in one database. You can read more about SQL Elastic pool and implementation from this blog post: `https://thuru.net/2015/10/04/` `azure-elastic-database-pool-managing-sql-databases-in-breeze/`

Accessing Azure SQL Database from SSMS

This is a fairly straightforward approach as latest versions of the SSMS have improved features in connecting and accessing SQL Databases. Find your database in the portal under the SQL Database category (Figure 2-12), and copy the server name.

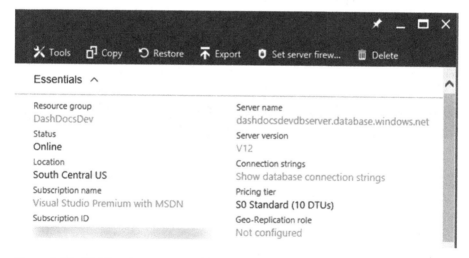

Figure 2-12. SQL Database overview blade

Go to SSMS and paste it in the server name section, select the authentication type as SQL Server Authentication, and enter the admin login credentials used to create the database server in the portal (Figure 2-13).

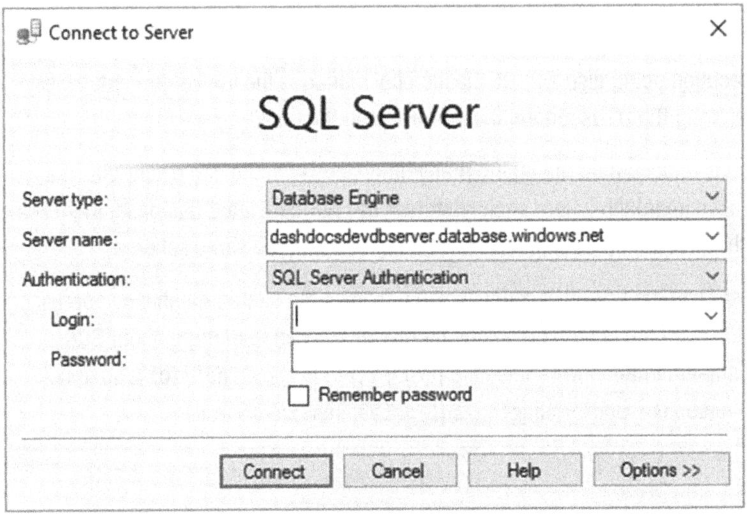

Figure 2-13. SSMS – Connect to Server window

You will get an error when trying to connect to the database server. This is because Azure SQL Database Servers are protected by a firewall that only allows the connections form the approved range of IP addresses.

In order to add your IP or IP range to the approved list, go to the database blade in the portal and click on the button 'Set server firewall' (Figure 2-14). It will open the firewall setting blade, and for convenience the blade will show the current IP address as well. Click on the 'Add client IP' on top and save. Now you can connect to the database from SSMS.

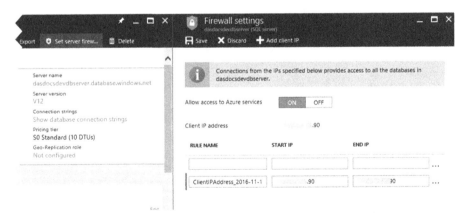

Figure 2-14. SQL Server Firewall settings

■ **Note**   Azure SQL Database IP settings are applied on the server level, not on the database level.

Entity Framework Code-First with Azure SQL Database

Code-First development experience with Azure SQL Database is analogous to the experience with the on-premises SQL Server database. In order to begin the application development with Azure SQL Database, we need the connection string. Copy the connection string of the database from the Azure portal and place it on the web.config.

In the database blade, you can see the connection string section and view it (Figure 2-15). When you click the 'Show database connection strings', the connection string blade (Figure 2-16) will show up. In this blade, you can get the connection string for various drivers.

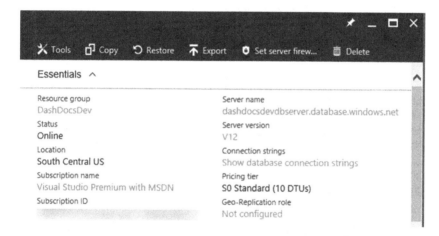

Figure 2-15. *Connection string settings in database overview blade*

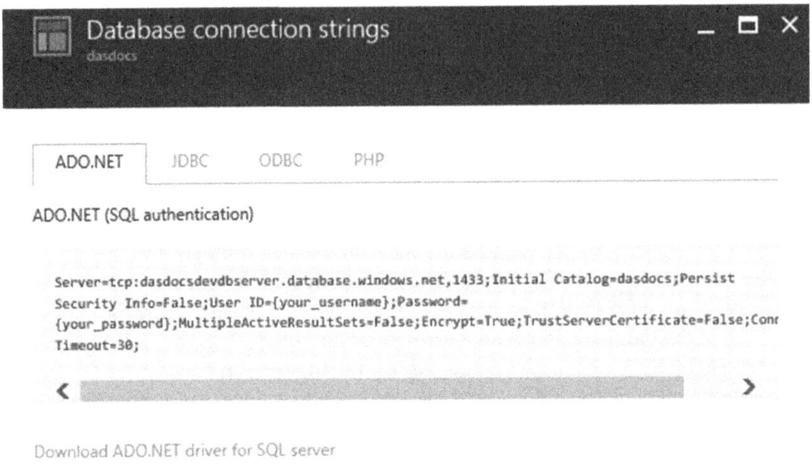

Figure 2-16. *Different connection string options*

We need ADO.NET connection string as we use Entity Framework. Copy the connection string and place it in the connection string section of the web.config.

```
<add name="DashDocsContext" connectionString="Server=tcp:dashdocsdevdbse
rver.database.windows.net,1433;Initial Catalog=dashdocs;Persist Security
Info=False;User ID=<USERNAME>;Password=<PASSWORD>;MultipleActiveResultSet
s=False;Encrypt=True;TrustServerCertificate=False;Connection Timeout=30;"
providerName="System.Data.SqlClient" />
```

Replace the username and the password in the connection string with the server admin login credentials created in the portal.

■ **Note** Here we use the server admin credentials in the connection string; but this is not a recommended practice in the production. We should use the credentials with at least enough permissions to run the application.

Creating the Code-First Models

We will create three simple model classes inside the Models folder in the web project. Before beginning we should install the Entity Framework (EF) to the project. In the Visual Studio Package Manager console enter the following command and install the latest version of EF.

```
Install-Package EntityFramework
```

Model classes are linked like this - **Customers** have many **Users** and one User can have many **Documents**. A user who uploads the document becomes the owner of the Document.

Customer.cs

```
public class Customer
{
    [Key]
    public Guid Id { get; set; }

    public string Name { get; set; }

    public virtual ICollection<User> Users { get; set; }
}
```

User.cs

```
public class User
{
    [Key]
    public Guid Id { get; set; }

    public string FirstName { get; set; }

    public string LastName { get; set; }

    [ForeignKey("Customer")]
    public Guid CustomerId { get; set; }

    [ForeignKey("CustomerId")]
    public virtual Customer Customer { get; set; }

    public virtual ICollection<Document> OwnedDocuments { get; set; }
}
```

Document.cs

```
public class Document
{
    [Key]
    public Guid Id { get; set; }
    public string DocumentName { get; set; }

    public DateTime CreatedOn { get; set; }

    [ForeignKey("Owner")]
    public Guid OwnerId { get; set; }
```

```
    public string BlobPath { get; set; }

    [ForeignKey("OwnerId")]
    public virtual User Owner { get; set; }

}
```

Once the models are created, add the context class (DashDocsContext.cs) inside a folder named Services.

DashDocsContext.cs

```
public class DashDocsContext : DbContext
{
    public DashDocsContext()
    {
    }

    public DbSet<Customer> Customers { get; set; }

    public DbSet<User> Users { get; set; }

    public DbSet<Document> Documents { get; set;}
}
```

In the Package Manager console enable EF code-first migration using the command below.

```
Enable-Migrations
```

Now we can add our first migration and update the database. Execute the command below in the Package Manager Console to create the first migration (named Initial) of the project.

```
Add-Migration Initial
```

After adding the first migration, we can see a file Configuration.cs created under the Migrations folder alongside the specific migration file (201612120708585_Initial.cs) with the suffix name Initial. Refer to Figure 2-17.

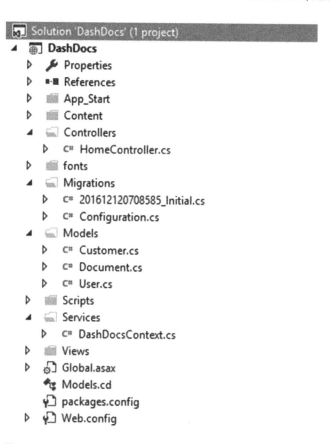

Figure 2-17. *Project structure*

Open Configuration.cs file add some seed data; we will add one customer record and two user records. This will be handy in starting the development and also viewing some data from the SQL Database before creating the actual code.

Replace the **Seed** method with the following one shown below - using ***AddOrUpdate*** using hard-coded Ids.

Configuration.cs

```
internal sealed class Configuration : DbMigrationsConfiguration<DashDocs.
Services.DashDocsContext>
    {
        public Configuration()
        {
            AutomaticMigrationsEnabled = false;
        }

        protected override void Seed(DashDocs.Services.DashDocsContext
        context)
```

```
    {
        Guid customerId = Guid.Parse("82CEAD1F-E3FA-4DAB-BFFA-
        276845FB7E72");

        Guid userIdKron = Guid.Parse("2A37108E-56AF-4C18-99C4-
        415191591CD9");
        Guid userIdTron = Guid.Parse("C22514F4-976E-48FD-AB3E-
        C12E945B3652");

        context.Customers.AddOrUpdate(
          c => c.Id,
          new Customer { Id = customerId, Name = "DashDocDevs" }
        );

        context.Users.AddOrUpdate(
            u => u.Id,
            new User { Id = userIdKron, FirstName = "Kron", LastName =
"Linda", CustomerId = customerId},
            new User { Id = userIdTron, FirstName = "Tron", LastName =
"Spagner", CustomerId = customerId}
            );

    }
  }
```

Now update the database with the first migration, by executing the command below. This will create the schema and populate the tables with the data in the Seed method.

```
Update-Database -verbose
```

Connect to the database using SSMS and check the schema and browse through the tables; you will see the database and the newly created tables (Customers and Users). These tables will have the hard-coded customer and user data from the seed method respectively.

Getting Started with Azure Blob Storage

Azure Blob Storage is part of the Azure Storage service. Azure Storage Service has four types of storages, namely, blobs, tables, queues, and file storage.

- **Blob storage** – Stores binary information; a blob can be any binary large object. Blob storage is also known as Object storage.

- **Table Storage** – Key-attribute type NoSQL-based persistence store. Effective and highly cost efficient.

- **Queues** – Provides reliable messaging for workflows and commonly used as a communication channel between web and worker roles of Azure Cloud Services.

- **File Storage** – Uses standard SMB protocol, offers shared file storage for legacy applications.

DashDocs manages documents, which are binary objects in terms of persistence, making Blob storage the best option for the use.

Creating an Azure Blob Storage

In the portal click 'New' and search for the Storage account. In the result blade (Figure 2-18), select the Storage account under the Storage category; Storage account under the VM Extensions category provides the storage for virtual hard disks of Azure virtual machines.

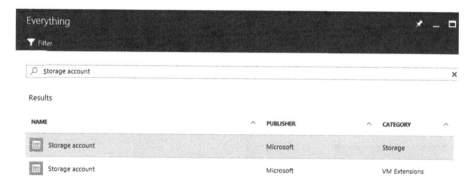

Figure 2-18. *Choosing Storage account*

Click 'Create' and this will open the Storage account creation blade (Figure 2-19).

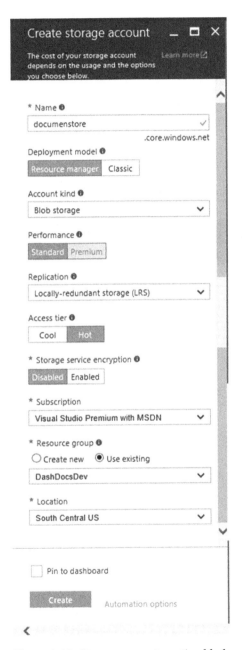

Figure 2-19. Storage account creation blade

Blob storage creation blade has many fields to be filled.

- **Name** – In the creation blade, give a name for the Blob storage. Based on the Azure storage naming convention, this name should be in lowercase (only letters and numbers are allowed) with the character limit between 3 and 24.

- **Deployment Model** – Select Azure Resource Manager as it is the latest deployment model and the way to go. Classic model is used for the storage accounts created using the old portal.

- **Account Kind** – Select Blob Storage. General purpose storage account provides storage for all four types (blobs, tables, queues, and files) in the same account, whereas Blob Storage account provides dedicated storage for blobs.

- **Performance** – Selecting the Account Kind as Blob Storage leaves this option locked in Standard. Standard allows the storage for blob storage and other storage services, where Premium performance tier facilitates disk storage with heavy IO workloads. It uses SSD for virtual machines.

- **Replication** – Choose Locally Redundant Storage (LRS) replication, since this is development storage. More about the storage replication is discussed in the next section.

- **Access Tier** – Having two options, Cool tier is used to store infrequently accessed data. Suitable for storing backups and file archives, this is priced lower compared to the Hot tier. Hot tier is the choice here, as it is used to store the frequently accessed data.

- **Storage Service Encryption** – Enabling this will allow Azure to encrypt the data at rest and automatically decrypt it when you access it. This is a basic in-built encryption mechanism, but still effective because this satisfies the organizational policies like keeping the data encrypted that stay outside the corporate firewall. Azure uses AED 256 encryption. Chapter 7 has details of security and encryption in greater detail. As of now you can leave this option disabled.

After completing the form, select the subscription, resource group (DashDocsDev) and a location, then click Create to deploy the Azure Blob Storage account.

Azure Blob Storage Replication

There are three different replication options available for Azure Blob Storage.

- **Locally Redundant Storage (LRS)** – Locally redundant storage maintains three copies of your data. LRS is replicated three times within a single data center in a single region. LRS protects your data from normal hardware failures, but not from the failure of a single datacenter.

- **Geo-Redundant Storage (GRS)** --GRS maintains six copies of your data. With GRS, your data is replicated three times within the primary region, and is also replicated three times in a secondary region hundreds of miles away from the primary region, providing the highest level of durability.

- **Read Access Geo-Redundant Storage (RAGRS)** – Read-access geo-redundant storage replicates your data to a secondary geographic location, and also provides read access to your data in the secondary location. Read-access geo-redundant storage allows you to access your data from either the primary or the secondary location.

Azure Blob Storage Structure

Storage account is the service boundary of the Azure Blob storage. Inside a blob storage account reside the containers. All the blobs are stored inside a container. Containers help to assign security policies as well.

In the portal, navigate to the storage account we created, and notice the icon to create containers (Figure 2-20). Click on that icon to create a container.

Figure 2-20. *Blob Storage overview blade with the '+ Container' icon*

In the container creation blade (Figure 2-21), notice there are three different options under the access types.

- **Private** – This is the default option; container and blob data can only be accessed by the account owner.

- **Blob** – Blobs inside the container can be accessed publicly without authentication.

- **Container** – Blob data can be accessed publicly without authentication and includes list permission to the container to list the blobs inside.

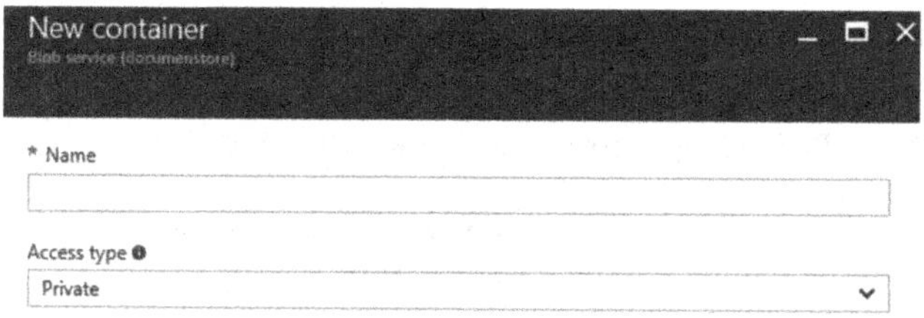

Figure 2-21. *New container creation blade*

Create a container named 'test' with a private access type. At the bottom of the storage account overview blade (Figure 2-20), you can see the list of containers and click on the 'test' container. This will open up the container blade that lists the blobs inside the container. This blade has a button on top to upload blobs. Click upload and it will open up the blob upload blade (Figure 2-22).

Figure 2-22. *Blob upload blade*

In the blob upload blade, notice there are three blob types listed in the drop-down.

- **Block blob** – Optimized for streaming and storing binary large objects in cloud Azure storage, making it the ideal choice for the documents, media files, etc.

- **Page blob** – Optimized for IaaS disks and supports random writes. Azure virtual machine network-attached IaaS disks are VHDs stored as page blobs.

- **Append blob** – Similar to block blobs, but optimized for append operations, making it the ideal choice for the log files, as they have frequent append operations.

Since block blob is the best option for storing documents, select the Block Blob option from the Blob Type drop-down and upload a document. You can see the uploaded file in the container blade.

Accessing Azure Blob Storage from SDK

In order to access the Azure storage account from our application, we need to authenticate to the service. Azure Blob Storage provides access keys to achieve authentication.

In the portal under the Blob Storage section find the option named Keys (Figure 2-23); there you will see the name of the blob storage account and two keys.

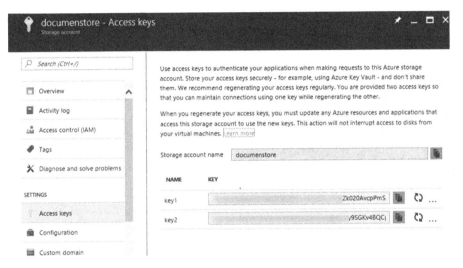

Figure 2-23. *Access Keys section of the blob storage*

One key is enough to access the storage, so let's construct the connection string for the Blob Storage and save it under the connection string section of the web.config. Replace the account name and the account key with the information found on the Access Keys blade shown in Figure 2-23.

```
<add name="DocumentStore" connectionString="DefaultEndpointsProtocol=https;A
ccountName=<ACCOUNT NAME>;AccountKey=<ACCOUNT KEY>"/>
```

■ **Note**　Generally APIs do offer more than one key in order to eliminate the downtime of the applications during the key regeneration. Applications do have the logic in place to connect/retry with the second key in case the first key fails. So, both keys wouldn't be regenerated at the same time: one will be regenerated and loaded into the application and then the second one will be generated.

As the settings are in place, let's create a simple file upload front end using ASP.MVC. Index.cshtml

```
<div class="col-md-12 no-padding">
          @using (Html.BeginForm("Upload", "Home", FormMethod.Post, new {
          enctype = "multipart/form-data" }))
          {
              <div class="form-group padding-top-25">
                      <label class="control-label ">Document</label>
                  <div class="col-md-12 no-padding">
                      <input type="file" name="document" id="document" />
                  </div>
              </div>

              <div class="form-group">
                  <div class="col-md-10 padding-tb-15">
                      <input type="submit" value="Upload" class="btn btn-
                      primary" />
                  </div>
              </div>
          }
      </div>
```

This simple form will post the file to the Upload action in Home controller. **Note that the CSS elements are not described in the book.**

Now let's add some code to upload the documents to the Azure Blob storage. First, install the Azure Storage SDK for .NET.

```
Install-Package WindowsAzure.Storage
```

Create a file called BlobStorageService.cs under the Services folder and add an UploadDocumentAsync method.

```
public async Task<string> UploadDocumentAsync(HttpPostedFileBase
documentFile, Guid customerId, Guid documentId)
      {
          var storageAccount = CloudStorageAccount.
          Parse(ConfigurationManager.ConnectionStrings["DocumentStore"].
          ConnectionString);
          var blobClient = storageAccount.CreateCloudBlobClient();

          var container = blobClient.GetContainerReference(customerId.
          ToString().ToLower());
          await container.CreateIfNotExistsAsync();

          var blobRelativePath = documentId.ToString().ToLower() + "/" +
          Path.GetFileName(documentFile.FileName).ToLower();

          var block = container.GetBlockBlobReference(blobRelativePath);

          await block.UploadFromStreamAsync(documentFile.InputStream);
          return blobRelativePath;
      }
```

As you see, the method UploadDocumentAsync gets three parameters: the uploaded file content, customer Id, and document Id.

It creates a container using the customer Id. (by default this will create a container with private access level) and uploads the document by appending the document Id in the blob reference path.

Creating separate containers for each customer helps in organizing the files of a customer in individual containers. But choosing the path in the Blob Storage is absolutely the choice of the developer. In large implementations, we create dedicated storage accounts for each customer as well. Also, appending a GUID, in this case the document Id to the file name and creating the document helps in not overriding any existing files.

In the HomeController.cs add an action named Upload.

```csharp
public async Task<ActionResult> Upload(HttpPostedFileBase document)
        {
            // Ids used in the seed method
            Guid customerId = Guid.Parse("82CEAD1F-E3FA-4DAB-BFFA-
            276845FB7E72");
            Guid userId = Guid.Parse("2A37108E-56AF-4C18-99C4-
            415191591CD9");

            var blobStorageService = new BlobStorageService();
            var documentId = Guid.NewGuid();

            var path = await blobStorageService.
            UploadDocumentAsync(document, customerId, documentId);

            var dbContext = new DashDocsContext();
            dbContext.Documents.Add(new Document
            {
                Id = documentId,
                DocumentName = Path.GetFileName(document.FileName).
                ToLower(),
                OwnerId = userId,
                CreatedOn = DateTime.UtcNow,
                BlobPath = path
            });
            await dbContext.SaveChangesAsync();

            return RedirectToAction("Index");
        }
```

The Upload Action performs two operations: it uploads the document to the Blob Storage and adds the document record to the SQL Database. Run the application and try uploading a document. Go to the Azure portal and browse your Blob Storage; you will see the container with the specified customer Id (Figure 2-24).

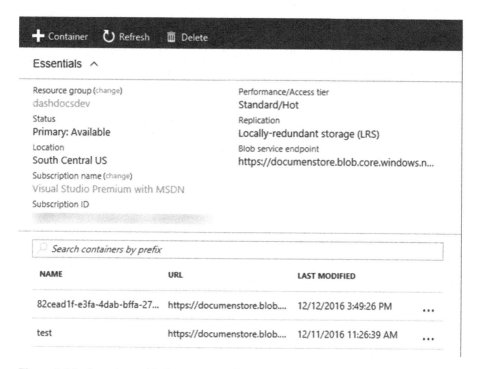

Figure 2-24. *Container with the customer Id*

Inside the container, you will see the uploaded documents (Figure 2-25). It shows a folder-like structure, the first folder with the document Id name; and when you navigate inside this folder you will see the uploaded document.

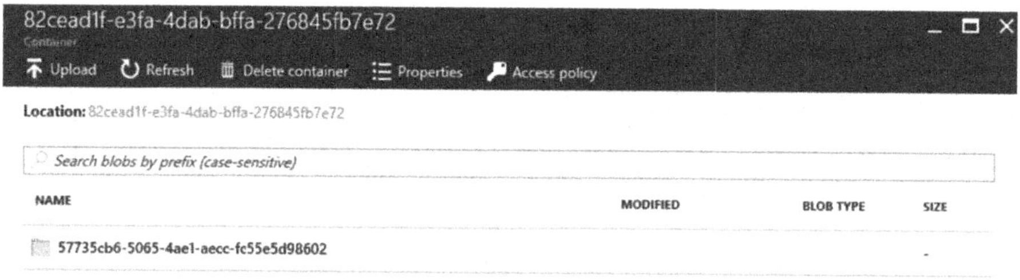

Figure 2-25. *Container listing*

Microsoft Azure Storage Explorer is a handy tool in managing the Azure Storage services. You can download the tool from this URL: `http://storageexplorer.com/`

▪ **Note**   The portal and other client tools used in managing the Blob storage visualize/
show the path elements of a block blob in a folder-file view. But technically Blob Storage
does not have a typical filesystem-like structure like the arrangement in our PCs. In Blob
Storage, everything is saved in a flat format.

In short, in the above activity you see the document Id as a folder and the uploaded
document inside that folder, but there is nothing called folder in the Blob Storage – the client
tools render the path in that way.

We should be able to download the documents we upload. Create a method named
DownloadDocumentAsync in the BlobStorageService class.

```
public async Task<KeyValuePair<string, MemoryStream>>
DownloadDocumentAsync(Guid documentId, Guid customerId)
        {
                var storageAccount = CloudStorageAccount.
                Parse(ConfigurationManager.ConnectionStrings["DocumentStore"].
                ConnectionString);
                var blobClient = storageAccount.CreateCloudBlobClient();

                var container = blobClient.GetContainerReference(customerId.
                ToString().ToLower());

                var dbContext = new DashDocsContext();
                var document = await dbContext.Documents.SingleAsync(d => d.Id
                == documentId);

                var block = container.GetBlockBlobReference(document.BlobPath);

                var stream = new MemoryStream();
                await block.DownloadToStreamAsync(stream);

                var content = new KeyValuePair<string, MemoryStream>(document.
                DocumentName, stream);

                return content;
        }
```

This method downloads the file content to a MemoryStream object. In order
to connect this with the DashDocs MVC application, add an action method named
Download, which takes document Id as a parameter.

```
public async Task<FileResult> Download(Guid documentId)
        {
                var dbContext = new DashDocsContext();
```

```
    var document = await dbContext.Documents.SingleAsync(d => d.Id
    == documentId);

    var blobStorageService = new BlobStorageService();
    var content = await blobStorageService.DownloadDocumentAsync(doc
    umentId, DashDocsClaims.CustomerId);

    content.Value.Position = 0;
    return File(content.Value, System.Net.Mime.MediaTypeNames.
    Application.Octet, content.Key);
}
```

Finalizing the First Version of DashDocs Application

Now our application has the features of uploading and downloading the documents. Let's add some simple logic to the Index action in the HomeController to list the documents of a customer. Note, the code uses the same hard-coded customer Id that was inserted during the migration process.

```
public async Task<ActionResult> Index()
    {
        Guid customerId = Guid.Parse("82CEAD1F-E3FA-4DAB-BFFA-
        276845FB7E72");

        var dbContext = new DashDocsContext();
        var documents = from document in dbContext.Documents
                        join user in dbContext.Users on document.OwnerId
                        equals user.Id
                        where user.CustomerId == customerId
                        select document;

        return View(documents.Include(d => d.Owner).ToList());
    }
```

Update the Index.cshtml with some Razor logic to display the information. The complete Index.cshtml is shown below.

Index.cshtml

```
@model IEnumerable<DashDocs.Models.Document>

<div class="col-md-12 bg-blue">
    @{
        ViewBag.Title = "DashDocs";
    }
```

```
</div>
    <div class="col-md-12 page-content">
        <div class="col-md-12 no-padding">
            @using (Html.BeginForm("Upload", "Home", FormMethod.Post, new {
            enctype = "multipart/form-data" }))
            {
                <div class="form-group padding-top-25">
                        <label class="control-label "> Upload your Doccument
                        : </label>
                    <div class="col-md-12 no-padding">
                        <input type="file" name="document" id="document" />
                    </div>
                </div>

                <div class="form-group">
                    <div class="col-md-10 padding-tb-15">
                        <input type="submit" value="Upload" class="btn btn-
                        primary" />
                    </div>
                </div>
            }
        </div>

        <div class="col-md-12 div-table">
            <h2>Recent Documents</h2>
            <table class="table table-hover">
                <tr>
                    <th>
                        Document Name
                    </th>
                    <th>
                        Owner
                    </th>
                    <th></th>
                </tr>
                <tbody>
                    @foreach (var item in Model)
                    {
                        <tr>
                            <td>
                                @Html.DisplayFor(modelItem => item.
                                DocumentName)
                            </td>
                            <td>
                                @Html.DisplayFor(modelItem => item.Owner.
                                FirstName)
                            </td>
                            <td>
```

```
                        @Html.ActionLink("Download", "Download", new
                        { documentId = item.Id })

                    </td>
                </tr>
            }
            </tbody>
        </table>

    </div>
</div>
```

After completing all the code, run the application and you will see a screen similar to Figure 2-26 (styles are not included in the book). Try uploading different documents and downloading them.

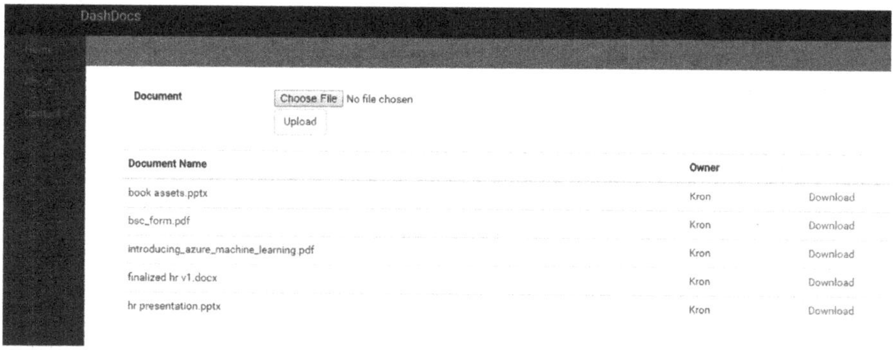

Figure 2-26. *DashDocs initial version*

Summary

In this chapter, we explored three fundamental Azure platform services and created the first version of the DashDocs application. Get the source code for this chapter from https://github.com/thuru/DashDocs/tree/master/DashDocs/Chapter%202.

Figure 2-27 shows the architecture overview of the DashDocs application at this point.

43

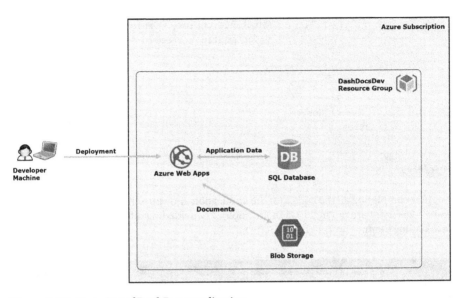

Figure 2-27. Overview of DashDocs application

CHAPTER 3

■ ■ ■

DevOps with Visual Studio Team Services and Azure

Delivery and flexibility are two highly demanded aspects of modern software development. Reaching the market quickly and responding to the changes quicker are the key factors of success. Collaboration between stakeholders and changing management and monitoring plays major roles in sustainable software delivery.

Visual Studio Team Services (VSTS) is a massive tool that has many facets and features required in a software development process, like project management, build automation, source control, environment management, collaboration, release management, etc.

VSTS is a big software service that supports Application Lifecycle Management (ALM) in greater depth. Covering all the features and services of VSTS is impossible; in this chapter we will cover the essential topics in a basic manner, in order to get started with VSTS and perform basic DevOps with Azure.

Getting Started with VSTS

VSTS is part of Azure Developer Tools services, **but it works as a stand-alone product as well**. You can reach the VSTS sign-up page from many links, but you will mostly have the same experience.

Go to the site https://www.visualstudio.com/team-services/ and click on any link that directs you to create a new VSTS account. You will land on a page that asks you to sign in with your Microsoft / Azure Active Directory account.

In order to keep the flow with the content of this book, let's take a very straightforward approach and use the same account credentials used in Chapter 1 to create the Azure account.

Setting Up a VSTS Account

Once you have signed in you will land on the page that guides you through the VSTS account creation process. On this web page (Figure 3-1) in the left-hand side, you will see your logged-in account details and the AAD directory. If your account is linked with more than one AAD, you will see a drop-down of them along with the option of Microsoft Account.

© Thurupathan Vijayakumar 2017
T. Vijayakumar, *Practical Azure Application Development*, DOI 10.1007/978-1-4842-2817-3_3

Thuru   Edit profile

vth@

| DashDocsDirectory | ∨ |

🌐

✉ vth@

Figure 3-1. VSTS account creation page – left side

In the above image, it displays my Microsoft Account and the list of directories the account is associated with. Choose the directory of the Azure account we created in Chapter 1. In this case it is the DashDocsDirectory, which is the default directory of the Azure account created in Chapter 1. This will help in keeping things aligned with the Azure account and make the integration smooth.

On the right-hand side of the web page, you see a similar section like as in Figure 3-2. Click on the 'Create new account' button to create a new VSTS account. See Figure 3-3.

Get started with Visual Studio Team Services

Services for teams to share code, track work, and ship software – for any language, all in a single package.

Create new account

Figure 3-2. VSTS account creation page – right side

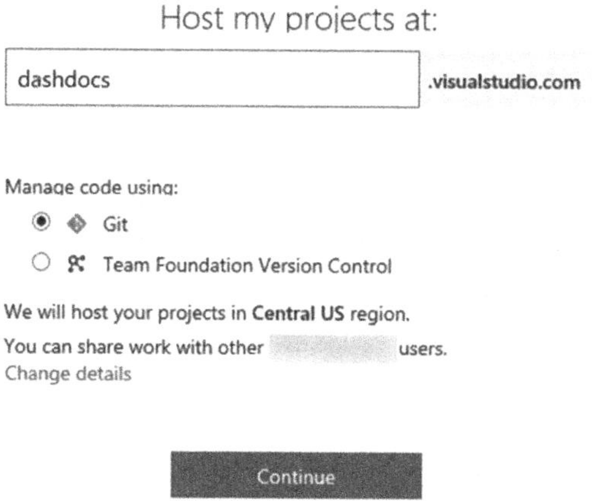

Host my projects at:

dashdocs   .visualstudio.com

Manage code using:

◉ ◈ Git

○ ✗ Team Foundation Version Control

We will host your projects in **Central US** region.
You can share work with other ▮▮▮▮▮ users.
Change details

Continue

Figure 3-3. Setting up VSTS account name and default protocol

Enter the name for the VSTS account (dashdocs.visualstudio.com), and select the source version management protocol. This is the default option setting for the sample project; later you can select Git or Team Foundation Version Control at the project level. Click 'Continue' and you will see the VSTS account provisioned with a sample project created for you.

Creating a Git Repo and Pushing the Code to VSTS

We have VSTS in place and now we have to publish the code to the Git repo. You should install the Git tools for Visual Studio 2015 in order to complete the following steps from Visual Studio.

Open your solution in the Visual Studio, right-click on the solution, and select 'Add Solution to Source Control...'. This will add the solution to a local Git repo. Then open Team Explorer tab (Figure 3-4).

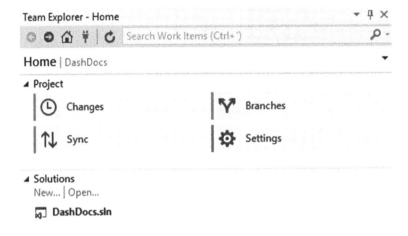

Figure 3-4. Team Explorer window

You can see the solution in Team Explorer (Figure 3-4); select the solution and click on the 'Sync' button on top. This will open the dialog (Figure 3-5) within the Team Explorer.

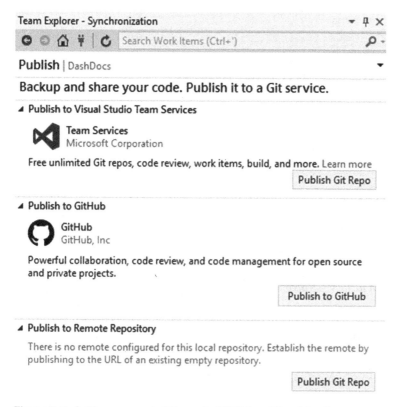

Figure 3-5. *Setting up remote Git repo in VSTS from Visual Studio*

Select the option 'Publish Git Repo' under the Publish to Visual Studio Team Services (the first section). If you are not signed in, log in to your VSTS using your account credentials (Figure 3-6).

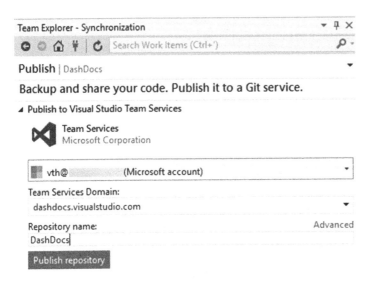

Figure 3-6. *Sign in to the VSTS account from Visual Studio*

This will populate the visual studio URL (choose the right one if you have more than one VSTS account associated with your account). Enter a name for your repository – DashDocs – and click 'Publish repository'. This will create a repository in your VSTS and push the code to the VSTS Git repo.

You can go the VSTS and navigate to the DashDocs repo and see the pushed code in the Code section.

■ **Note**   VSTS and Git are vast technologies; this book only covers what is required to begin the development using those technologies. In a real project, the VSTS settings and user permissions vary to a greater degree. As an enterprise developer, sometimes you might not get the chance to administer the VSTS account with full permissions. The steps mentioned here do not necessarily adhere to any enterprise standards or best practices of ALM.

Creating Build Definition and Deployment to Azure Web Apps

In the DashDocs repo of the VSTS, click on the 'Builds & Releases' tab option. You will see the screen like the one in Figure 3-7. Click on the 'New definition' button to create a new build definition.

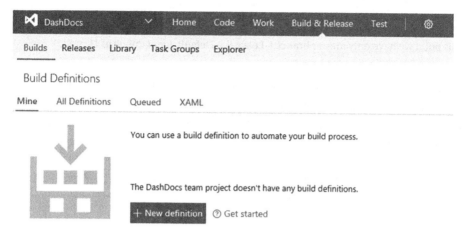

Figure 3-7. *Builds and Releases page view*

'Create new build definition' dialog will show up (Figure 3-8), select the Deployment tab, and select the 'Azure Web App' option and click 'Next'. This template creates the build and configure Continuous Integration (CI) and Continuous Deployment (CD) setup for the application.

Figure 3-8. *Create new build definition dialog*

After clicking 'Next' you will see a similar dialog (Figure 3-9) where we can select the source repo and create the build definition. Select the project and the branch (master – at this point we have only master branch). Leave the Default agent queue as Hosted.

■ **Note**   Build Agents are used in building the code, so we can use Default agents that are private agents we set up to build our code. Private agents give customized control in the build process since we can configure them with the custom software. Hosted agents are preconfigured build agents available in VSTS. Hosted agents are mostly sufficient for most of the code base. You can check the software configuration of the Hosted agents from this link: https://www.visualstudio.com/en-us/docs/build/concepts/agents/hosted#software

---

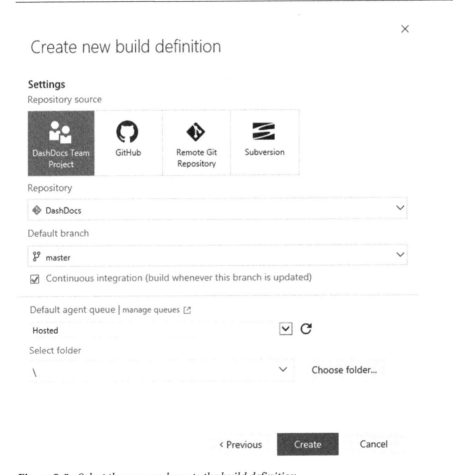

Figure 3-9. *Select the repo and create the build definition*

Click 'Create' and complete the creation of the build definition. This will create the build definition from the selected template (Azure Web Apps) and take you there.

In the newly constructed build definition we need to fill the right parameters and connections in order to make things work. The created build definition has six steps (Figure 3-10).

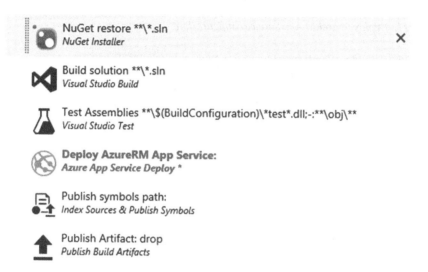

Figure 3-10. *Default steps of the Azure Web App Deployment template*

We do not need any additional steps to build our application. We have a simple ASP MVC application; we will build it using the existing build template and deploy it to the Azure Web Apps. Let's see what each of these steps performs.

The first step is NuGet restore, in the second step the agent builds the solution, then it runs the tests from any existing tests projects in the third step. The fourth step deploys the application to the Azure Web App using Azure Resource Manager deployment.

The fifth step (Publish symbols path) enables you to use the .pdb symbol files to debug the application on a machine other than the one you used to build the app. The last step (Publish Artifact) publishes the output of the build process to the specific path.

The fourth step 'Deploy AzureRM App Service' stays red because we need to configure it. Select 'Deploy AzureRM App Service' step (Figure 3-11). We need to fill two fields in order to make this step work.

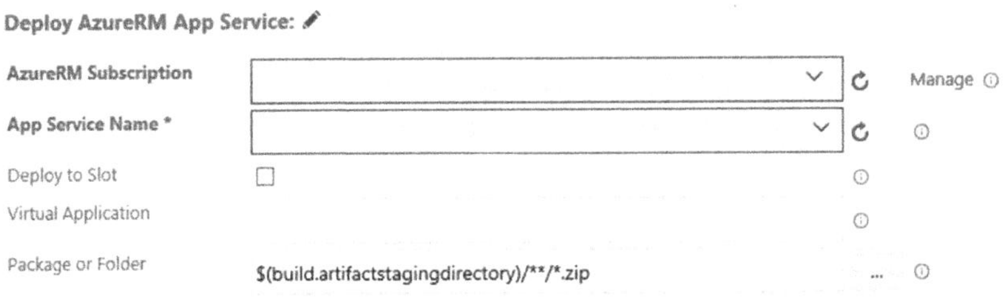

Deploy AzureRM App Service: ✏

AzureRM Subscription		⌄ ↻	Manage ⓘ
App Service Name *		⌄ ↻	ⓘ
Deploy to Slot	☐	↻	ⓘ
Virtual Application			ⓘ
Package or Folder	$(build.artifactstagingdirectory)/**/*.zip	...	ⓘ

Figure 3-11. *Deploy AzureRM App Service configuration*

Click the drop-down and you will see your Azure subscription. Select the subscription, then click on the App Service Name drop-down, and you will see the list of App Service Apps in the subscription (Figure 3-12). Select the dashdocs-dev Web App and leave the other settings as default. Save the build definition and give a name to it (Figure 3-13).

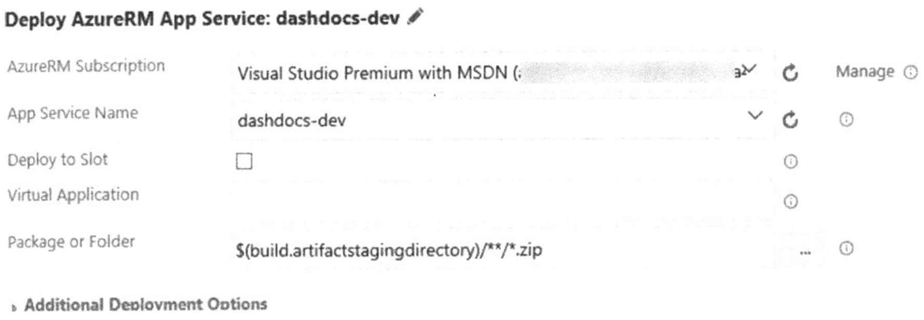

Deploy AzureRM App Service: dashdocs-dev ✏

AzureRM Subscription	Visual Studio Premium with MSDN (⁑	⌄ ↻	Manage ⓘ
App Service Name	dashdocs-dev	⌄ ↻	ⓘ
Deploy to Slot	☐		ⓘ
Virtual Application			ⓘ
Package or Folder	$(build.artifactstagingdirectory)/**/*.zip	...	ⓘ

▸ Additional Deployment Options

Figure 3-12. *Select the subscription and App Service from the drop-down*

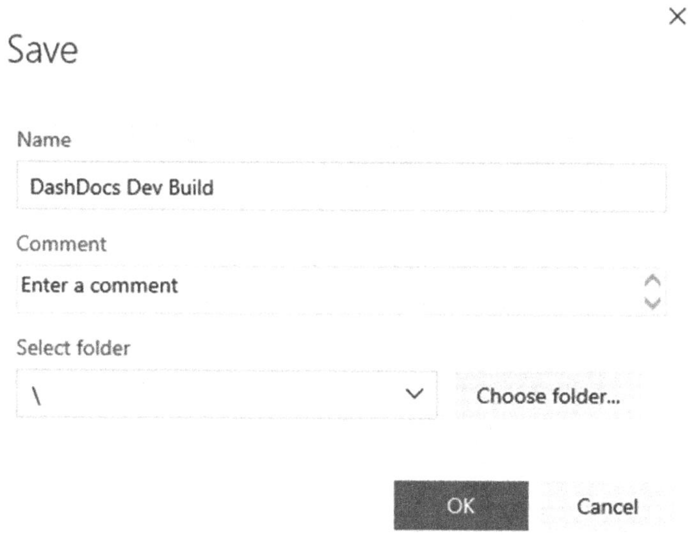

×

Save

Name

DashDocs Dev Build

Comment

Enter a comment

Select folder

\   ∨   Choose folder...

OK   Cancel

Figure 3-13. *Save the build definition*

You can see the options in the drop-down without any additional settings because we created the VSTS account with the AAD directory account, which has the subscription administrator permissions. **If you're using a VSTS account that is not linked with the Azure account, then you should configure the required service endpoints to access the Azure account.**

___

■ **Note**   All the build steps can be configured in greater depth and customized to suit the project and build requirements. But this chapter focuses on the simple getting-started model of VSTS and Azure deployment and skips the customization of the build steps. The out-of-the-box build template does the required work here.

___

After saving the build definition, click on the 'Queue new build' option on top and click 'OK' in the dialog window to test the build definition. This will launch the first build in VSTS and deploy the site to the Azure Web App. You can see the build steps and detailed logs on the screen (Figure 3-14).

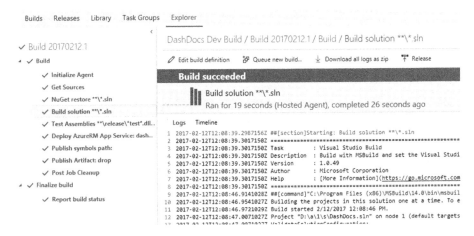

Figure 3-14. *Build process and logs in VSTS*

Since we didn't change the default options, this build definition has the continuous integration check-in trigger - it will build the solution whenever there's a push made to the Git repo.

Enabling Application Monitoring Using Azure Application Insights

Azure Application Insights is a comprehensive service that monitors and tracks various telemetries of the application. It also has the proactive alerts that will be triggered before the actual incident occurs. We can extend Application Insights to meet custom application monitoring and logging requirements as well.

In the Azure portal, search for Application Insights (Figure 3-15) and add a new Application Insights resource to the existing DashDocsDev resource group.

Figure 3-15. *Choose Application Insights*

Select the Application Insights and click create. This will open the Application Insight creation blade (Figure 3-16). Name the new Application Insights, and leave the application type as ASP.NET Application. Note that Application Insights support the Java applications, Hockey App integration, and other general applications as well.

Figure 3-16. *Application Insights creation blade*

Once the creation of the Application Insights is done, we need to configure the integration of the DashDocs application with the Application Insights resource.

First, in the Azure portal, navigate to the created Application Insights resource and copy the Instrumentation Key (Figure 3-17); this is the key used to identify the specific Application Insights instance.

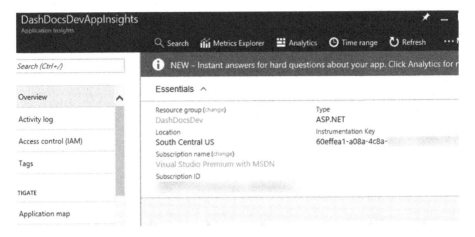

Figure 3-17. Application Insights Instrumentation Key

Place the key in the app settings section of the ***web.config*** of DashDocs application.

```
<add key="appInsight:InstrumentationKey" value="<INSTRUMENTATION KEY>" />
```

Install the Application Insights NuGet reference for the ASP.NET web applications.

```
Install-Package Microsoft.ApplicationInsights.Web
```

Place the following line of code in the ***Global.asax*** - Application_Start method.

```
TelemetryConfiguration.Active.InstrumentationKey = WebConfigurationManager.
AppSettings["appInsight:InstrumentationKey"];
```

Now the DashDocs application will send telemetry data to the Application Insights, and you should be able to see the data in the portal.

Run the application in the local machine (you can simply run the application in debug mode from Visual Studio) and perform some actions or refreshes and check the Application Insights section in the Azure portal; you will see the collected telemetry data (Figure 3-18).

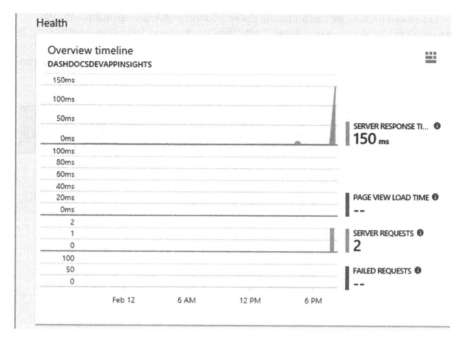

Figure 3-18. *Application Insights Telemetry*

■ **Note**   You log custom exceptions messages to the Application Logs and use it not only as a telemetry and monitoring service but also as a custom application logging service.

Automate Azure Environment Provisioning Using Azure Resource Manager (ARM) Templates

In a well-streamlined enterprise, application development setup has more than one environment. Environments for dev, testing, staging, and production are some common ones; in certain cases, we can see more complex and additional environments in the DevOps pipeline.

Azure Resource Manager (ARM) provides the ability create the infrastructure-as-code in JSON format - these JSON templates are known as ARM templates. ARM templates have high degree of customization and automation. They also support incremental- and change-based resource provisioning as well, which makes ARM templates a solid choice for the Azure infrastructure automation.

Azure provides an easy template generation and execution experience in the portal itself. Additionally, you can use PowerShell, custom code with Azure Management APIs, Azure REST APIs, or any other third-party tools to generate and execute the ARM templates.

Let's focus on how we can automate the provisioning of Azure environments. We have our development resource group 'DashDocsDev', and now let's create another environment for the DashDocs application.

In the Azure portal, navigate to the development resource group 'DashDocsDev' and you will the see an option named 'Automation script' under the Settings section (Figure 3-19).

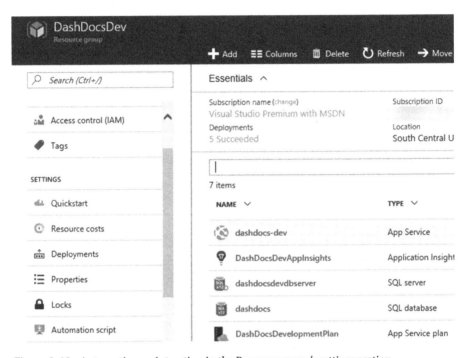

Figure 3-19. *Automation script option in the Resource group's settings section*

Click on the 'Automation script' option and this will open a blade with the automation. **Note that different execution options of the ARM template are listed in different tabs** (Figure 3-20).

Figure 3-20. ARM template blade

In the ARM template, you can see the options of variables and parameters. The template generator is capable enough to identify the parameters like resource names, SKU type (pricing tier), and other resource-specific configurations and add them as parameters, which will require external input. This requires greater flexibility in customizing the ARM templates.

You can download the template and save it for later use; in this case we will deploy this template directly from the Azure portal. Click on the Deploy button and it will open the deployment blade (Figure 3-21).

■ **Note**   ARM templates can be configured to take the input parameters from an output value of a resource. For example, if we're to add a connection string of a database to a web application's application settings section, this can be configured in the ARM template using the parameters and variables. Provisioning resources from an ARM template creates only the resource, NOT the content of the resource. For example, the new database that will be provisioned when executing the script will NOT have the data from the development database.

TEMPLATE

▦ 10 resources

✎ Edit   ⓘ Learn more

BASICS

* Subscription	Visual Studio Premium with MSDN ⌄
* Resource group ❶	⦿ Create new ○ Use existing
* Location	South Central US ⌄

SETTINGS

Alertrules_Failure_Anomalies__Dash Docs Dev App Insights_name	Failure Anomalies - DashDocsProdAppInsights
Components_Dash Docs Dev App Insights_name	DashDocsProdAppInsights
Servers_dashdocsdevdbserver_name	dashdocsproddbserver
Storage Accounts_documenstore_name	dashdocsprodstore
Serverfarms_Dash Docs Development Plan_name	DashDocsProductionPlan
Sites_dashdocs_dev_name	dashdocsprod ✓
Databases_dashdocs_name	dashdocsproddbserver/dashdocsprod
Databases_master_name	dashdocsproddbserver/master
Firewall Rules_allow_all_name	dashdocsproddbserver/allow all
Firewall Rules_Allow All Windows Azure Ips_name	dashdocsproddbserver/AllowAllWindowsAzureIps

TERMS AND CONDITIONS

Azure Marketplace Terms │ Azure Marketplace

By clicking "Purchase," I (a) agree to the applicable legal terms associated with the offering; (b) authorize Microsoft to charge or bill my current payment method for the fees associated the offering(s), including applicable taxes, with the same billing frequency as my Azure subscription, until I discontinue use of the offering(s); and (c) agree that, if the deployment involves 3rd party offerings, Microsoft may share my contact information and other details of such deployment with the publisher of that offering.

☐ I agree to the terms and conditions stated above

Figure 3-21. *Deployment blade*

In the deployment blade, under the Basics section, you can select the subscription, create a new resource group, or use any existing resource group and select the location of the resource group to deploy.

Under the Settings section, we have to fill the names and other details to create the resources. Tick the check box on the bottom and agree to the purchase statement of the mentioned resources. Click 'Purchase', and this will begin the deployment of the new resources.

■ **Note** ARM templates have default options most of the options. You can see that in the generated template as well. One of the main aspects of these default options is the SKU level, which determines the price and service capacity of the respective services. You can alter the template and set the required parameters before the deployment.

Handling Environment Settings in Web Apps

Creating different environments produces different settings for the resources, like connection strings and access keys will be different from the ones used in the development environment.

Azure Web Apps provides a handy feature in the portal itself, and we can use the 'Application settings' of a Web App to override the settings (both connection strings and app settings) during runtime. This saves us from putting additional effort in creating web. config translations.

Navigate to the Web App and click on the 'Application settings'. It will open the App settings blade (Figure 3-22).

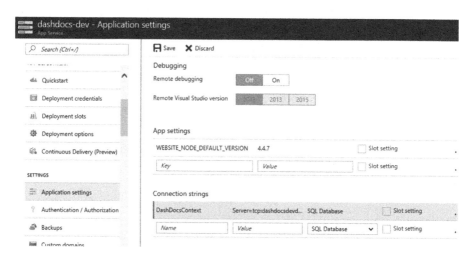

Figure 3-22. *Application settings of the Web App*

The values provided here will override the values of the connection strings and app settings with the same key in the web.config.

Summary

We configured several aspects of the DevOps – Added the solution to a Git repo in VSTS, enabled Continuous Integration (CI) and Continuous Deployment (CD), and enabled application monitoring using Application Insights. We also provisioned another environment for DashDocs application using the ARM template. Get the source code for this chapter from `https://github.com/thuru/DashDocs/tree/master/DashDocs/Chapter%203`.

Up to the completion of Chapter 3, the DashDocs application has had an architectural overview like the below illustration (Figure 3-23). The image shows the development environment.

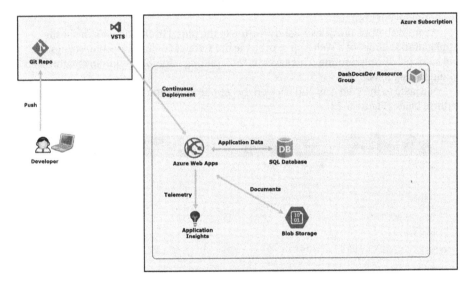

Figure 3-23. *Overview of the DashDocs application*

CHAPTER 4

■ ■ ■

Azure Active Directory and Multitenancy

Based on the general definition available in the web sphere, software multitenancy is defined as – "single instance of software serving multiple tenants, where a tenant is defined as group of users sharing common access and privileges." Though it is pragmatically hard to define what a single software instance is, it is quite common in the industry to address solutions as multitenant solutions based on their capabilities of handling different group of users; in enterprise SaaS solutions, often these groups are either different organizations or different departments.

When it comes to Azure, Azure Active Directory (AAD) is known as a tenant. So, in terms of Azure, multitenancy can be considered as enabling access to the application from different AADs. AAD being part of other Microsoft services facilitates the login experience of various other third-party SaaS applications, and integration with the AAD gives the benefit of single sign-on as well.

AAD and Azure Login Experience

First, let's focus on the role AAD plays in Azure. You can get an AAD by acquiring any of these following Microsoft cloud services such as Azure, Microsoft Intune, or Office 365. **This reveals that AAD is not an inherent part or feature of Azure alone.** It is the common authentication and identity service for other Microsoft cloud services as well.

On the other side of the spectrum, **Azure trusts only AAD as its authentication provider.** Syncing an on-premises Active Directory (AD) with an AAD allows the organizations to extend the identity management to the cloud. This enables single sign-on with many cloud applications.

Microsoft Account Login

In Chapter 1, we used a consumer email address to purchase an Azure account and create the subscription. In fact, the account administrator credential is a Microsoft Account, yet we are able to log in to Azure and perform operations. This contradicts the statement that Azure allows the authentications only through AAD.

© Thurupathan Vijayakumar 2017
T. Vijayakumar, *Practical Azure Application Development*, DOI 10.1007/978-1-4842-2817-3_4

We are able to log in to Azure using the assigned Microsoft Account because, **AAD trusts the Microsoft Account identity provider.**

Using your credentials (you should have the credentials of a user who is a subscription admin with Global Admin role in your directory), log in to the new portal and navigate to the AAD section (Figure 4-1).

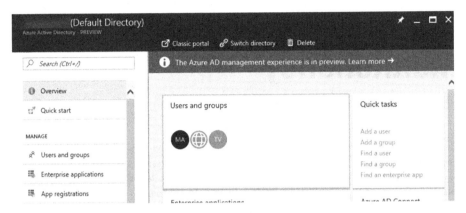

Figure 4-1. *AAD overview in the new portal*

Under the users of the AAD, you will see the Microsoft Account you used to log in. This explains how the authentication to Azure, from a Microsoft Account gets validated.

Creating an AAD User

Since we have an AAD tenant, which was created by default during the Azure account provisioning process (this directory is named as Default Directory), let's create a new user in our AAD.

Click on the 'Users and groups' section (Figure 4-1) to create a new user. This will open the user's blade (Figure 4-2), click the 'Add' button on top of the blade. This will open the user creation blade (Figure 4-3).

Figure 4-2. *AAD users blade*

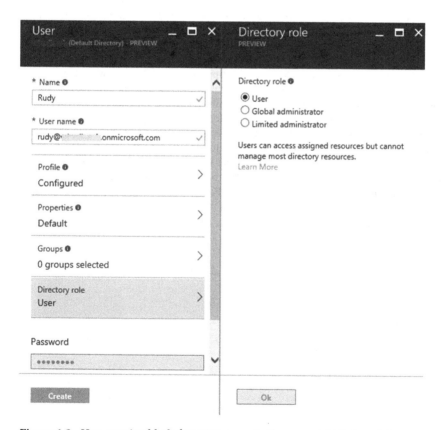

Figure 4-3. *User creation blade (creating a user in the current AAD domain)*

Enter the name of the user, and enter <username>@<your domain>.onmicrosoft.com in the User name section.

At this point, the domain is calculated like this:

1. If your account administrator credential is linda@outlook.com then your domain becomes lindaoutlook.

2. The username would be rudy@lindaoutlook.onmicrosoft.com.

You can see your corresponding domain on top of the user creation blade, right under the header 'User' (which is blurred in Figure 4-3).

■ **Note** When you create your Azure account, the AAD gets provisioned with the default domain, which is the username (email address) of the account administrator. Later you can add custom domains to your AAD to create users in the format of user@yourdomain.com.

Continuing with the user creation process, you can enter the details of the user in the Profile section. In the Properties section, you would notice that the source of authority is Azure Active Directory since this is a user account provisioned in the AAD itself - meaning this is neither a Microsoft Account nor a local AD user account synced with AAD.

Back to the user creation blade, leave the Groups section as it is, since we haven't created any groups. Select 'User' as the Directory Role (this is the default option). Last you can see a generated password; make sure you copy the password since there's no real email delivery available for the user we created at this point (user will be prompted to change the password during the first login). Click 'Create' and complete the user creation process.

At this point, if the newly created user logs in to https://portal.azure.com she will see an empty portal experience and when she tries to create the resources, she will be prompted by a message very similar to Figure 4-4, because this user is not allocated to any Azure roles yet. The Role Based Access Control (RBAC) section of this chapter describes about role assignment and resource management

Figure 4-4. *Empty portal experience*

■ **Note** Just adding the users to AAD without any permissions to the Azure would give them the empty portal experience in the new portal URL. But if the same users try to access the classic portal, they will be treated with a message saying no subscription allocated to the current user.

Inviting External Users to AAD

In the user creation blade (Figure 4-3) you can enter any valid email address as the username, but when you enter an email address that is outside the current AAD domain, **the blade will reflect that the user can be added as a guest** (Figure 4-5).

Figure 4-5. *Creating a guest user*

You can notice the Directory Role section and the password generation is no longer visible in this mode, because this is an external user; first this user account needs to be translated into a Microsoft Account, then only it becomes a valid AAD user authority. **Guest accounts are translated into Microsoft Accounts and then become the AAD accounts**.

Create a guest account with any of your custom emails, and once the user is created the external user will receive an AAD invitation with the custom message entered, similar to what is shown in Figure 4-6.

Figure 4-6. Invitation to Guest users from AAD

When the user clicks on the link in the email, she will be directed to the page similar to what is shown in Figure 4-7.

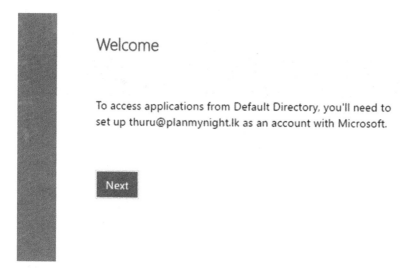

Figure 4-7. Process to set up the external user account as Microsoft Account

Following the steps would lead the user to translate the external email to a Microsoft Account. Once the Microsoft Account has been set up, the rest of the process is the same as a typical AAD user login.

In the next section, we'll look into the details of how to assign the Azure permissions to these users. As of now they ae just members of the AAD and do not have any permissions inside the Azure subscription.

Role Based Access Control (RBAC)

We created the users in AAD using different options; now those users can log in to Azure portal but will have the empty portal experience as shown in Figure 4-4.

Assigning them to roles of various resources would give them access to the respective resources with the respective permissions. This mechanism is known as Azure Role Based Access Control (RBAC). There are various built-in Azure roles available with different permission levels. You can read more about the different built-in roles and permissions from this link: `https://docs.microsoft.com/en-us/azure/active-directory/role-based-access-built-in-roles`. Apart from the built-in roles we can create custom roles as well. You can read more about the custom roles from this link: `https://docs.microsoft.com/en-us/azure/active-directory/role-based-access-control-custom-roles`.

Assigning Resources to the Users

Let's assign some resource permissions to the users we created in the previous section. We need to add Rudy to the development resource group (DashDocsDev) as she is one of the developers. Navigate to the resource group and select 'Access control (IAM)' as shown in Figure 4-8.

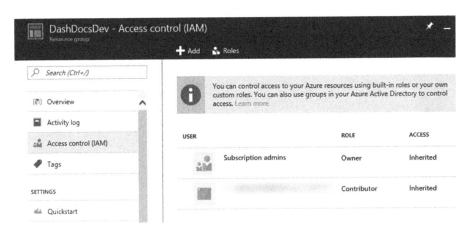

Figure 4-8. *Assign user to a resource group (RBAC)*

Click the 'Add' button on top of the blade, and this will open the blade shown in Figure 4-9. First, select the role as Contributor – **contributors have all the access to the specified resources except managing access to the resource**, then select the user and create the role based access control.

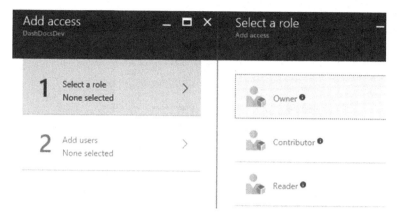

Figure 4-9. *Adding RBAC to a user*

Now log in to the portal using the credentials of the user. You will see the resources of the DashDocsDev resource group. Since the user is in the Contributor role, she is permitted to add and remove resources from the specified resource group as well.

■ **Note**   RBAC is an advanced concept and the above topic covered the very basic aspects of it.

Enabling Multitenancy with AAD

In Azure terms, an Azure Active Directory (AAD) is known as an Azure tenant, allowing AAD authentication to an application and configuring it to accept the authentications from different AADs, making an application multitenant from the AAD perspective.

A user logged into her Office 365 account via AAD is not required to enter her credentials to log in to another application that uses the authentication from the same AAD.

Applications being multitenanted that accept authentication from AADs gain the advantage of single-sign-on (SSO) during the scenarios like above.

Setting Up the AAD Application in the Portal

In order to create or enable AAD based multitenancy in an application, first we need to register an application in AAD. **The AAD where the application is registered becomes the owner directory of the application and is known as the home tenant**.

When other AADs authenticate to your application they have to trust the owning AAD (home tenant) and grant the access requested by the application.

Let's enable the AAD authentication in the DashDocs application. Go to the Azure portal and navigate to the Azure Active Directory section – assuming your credential has the Global Admin role in the AAD. Click on the 'App registrations' link in the AAD overview blade (Figure 4-10).

Figure 4-10. *AAD overview blade and app registrations section*

In the right-hand side, you can see the apps registered with your AAD. Click 'Add' to create a new app in the AAD (Figure 4-11).

Figure 4-11. *Register new AAD application*

Enter a name for the application and select the application type as Web app/API. If you're developing a desktop application, you can select the Native option. In the Sign-on URL section, enter any valid URL pattern; this URL does not need to be an existing one. Finally click 'Create' and complete the AAD app registration process.

After the creation, the app will be listed under the 'app registrations' section of the AAD overview blade (Figure 4-10).

Click on the newly created app and it will open up the application overview and settings blade (Figure 4-12).

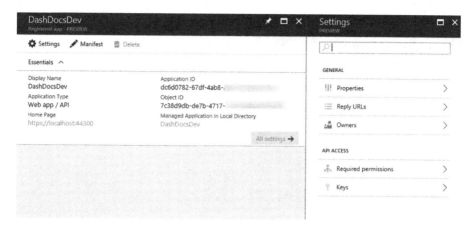

Figure 4-12. *Application overview and settings blade*

You can see the Application ID and the Object ID. Application ID is the public identifier of this app and Object ID is the identifier assigned to this application by the AAD in its object directory.

Click on the 'Properties' section in the right-hand side, and this will open the application properties blade (Figure 4-13).

Figure 4-13. *AAD application properties*

In the application properties blade, you can edit the name of the application and add a logo. Also, set the Multitenanted option to 'Yes' – **which indicates that this app is allowed to handle authentications through external AADs other than the home tenant as well**.

Copy the application ID and keep it; we will use this later in the code. Click 'Save' to save the changes.

■ **Note** When we create an application in the AAD, technically it creates two objects. One is the Application Object that is identified by the application ID and the global representation of the app situated in the home tenant. Azure AD Graph application entity defines the application object. (`https://msdn.microsoft.com/Library/Azure/Ad/Graph/api/entity-and-complex-type-reference#application-entity`)

Other one is the Service Principal object, which defines the policy and the permissions for an application. This acts as the basis for the required security principal and represents the application in runtime. The service principal object is the local representation of the application. Azure AD Graph service principal entity defines the service principal object. (`https://msdn.microsoft.com/Library/Azure/Ad/Graph/api/entity-and-complex-type-reference#serviceprincipal-entity`)

In order for an AAD application to access the resources, a service principle object should be created in the respective AAD. A single-tenant application will have the application object and the service principal object in the home tenant, and the multitenant application will have its application object in the home tenant and service principal objects in each AAD that has given the consent to access the resources.

Therefore, an application object has a 1:1 mapping with the application and service principle object has 1:n mapping with the application having one instance in each different AAD.

Back in the application overview and settings blade (Figure 4-12), click on the 'Reply URLs'; this will open the blade to configure the reply URLs of the application (Figure 4-14).

An application can have more than one reply URL, after the login AAD will redirect to the specified URL in the HTTP request. When a client makes an OAuth request to the AAD, it sends the reply URL the HTTP requests, and the sent reply URL should be in the list of reply URLs configured here; otherwise AAD will not redirect to the requested URL.

Figure 4-14. *Reply URLs blade*

In the Reply URL blade, add `https://localhost:44300` to test the application in during the development (we will configure this in the DashDocs project application in Visual Studio). Also, add the URL of the hosted application, in this case `https://dashdocs-dev.azurewebsites.net/` as this is required for the deployed application to work. We can do the mapping through the Application Settings section of the Web Apps described in Chapter 3.

AAD Authentication Flow and App Permissions

When a user enters her AAD credentials (AAD username and the password) and signs in, first the credentials are validated by the respective AAD. After the successful validation, the respective **AAD will return the id_token and the authentication code. The id_token is signed by the issuer (respective AAD) and it is a JSON Web Token (JWT).**

The id_token contains the basic profile information of the logged-in user along with the information of the token issuer. An authentication code will be used to request the access_token. The access_token will be issued based on the requested permissions by the service principal.

These permissions are configured in the application object in the home tenant by the developer. Though the developer can request for all the permissions, most of permissions require the consent to be granted only by the administrator of the AAD due to the sensitivity of the data and operations access that could be performed by the requested permission.

Let's see the permissions requested by our application we created in AAD. Navigate to the AAD section and go to the 'Application registrations' (Figure 4-10) and select the DashDocsDev application.

This will open the application overview and settings blade (Figure 4-13). In the right-hand section click on 'Required permissions' and this will open the Required permissions blade (Figure 4-15).

Figure 4-15. *Required permissions blade*

The 'Required permissions' blade (Figure 4-15) has the list of APIs that the DashDocsDev application requires access to. Note that AAD API has already been added to the list. We can add other APIs like AAD Graph API, Office 365 API and any other application or service principal that has the AAD authentication.

Click on the AAD API and this will open the blade (Figure 4-16) that lists the permissions the application requests against the selected API. In this list, the permissions fall under two categories.

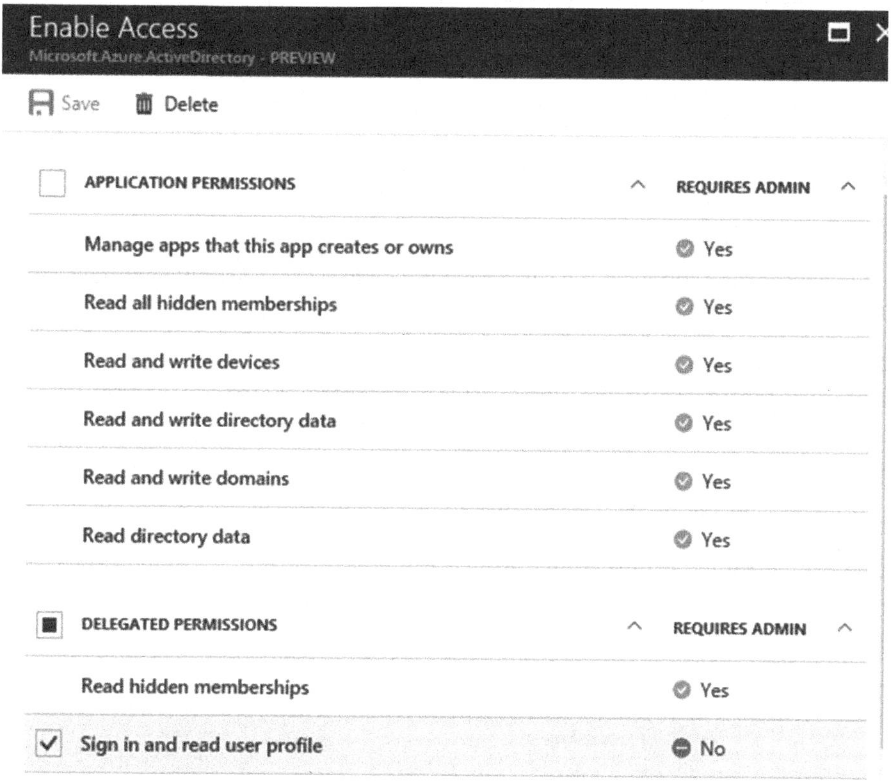

Enable Access
Microsoft.Azure.ActiveDirectory - PREVIEW

🔲 Save   🗑 Delete

APPLICATION PERMISSIONS	REQUIRES ADMIN
Manage apps that this app creates or owns	✔ Yes
Read all hidden memberships	✔ Yes
Read and write devices	✔ Yes
Read and write directory data	✔ Yes
Read and write domains	✔ Yes
Read directory data	✔ Yes

DELEGATED PERMISSIONS	REQUIRES ADMIN
Read hidden memberships	✔ Yes
✔ Sign in and read user profile	➖ No

Figure 4-16. *Application permissions blade*

They are the Application permissions and the Delegated permissions.

1. Application Permissions – Application permissions are used when the application access the resources by itself.

2. Delegated Permissions – Delegated permissions are used by the logged in user.

Applications can have keys - you can notice the keys section in the application overview blade (Figure 4-12) and these keys are used to authenticate to the AAD as the application and perform operations; in this scenario the permissions granted for the application will be used. When a user logged in using the application, the delegated permissions will be used as the operations will be carried out by the user.

■ **Note**   We will use the default permissions and the AAD authorization flow with the id_token. Requesting the access_token and performing other operations including querying broad areas and you can read more about that from this link: `https://docs.microsoft.com/en-us/azure/active-directory/develop/active-directory-graph-api-quickstart`.

Configuring the MVC Application to Use AAD Authentication

Let's configure and add some code to our application to enable AAD authentication. First, add the required settings in the web.config under the app settings section.

```
<add key="ClientAppId" value="<APPLICATION ID>" />
<add key="Authority" value="https://login.microsoftonline.com/common" />
<add key="ReplyUrl" value="https://localhost:44300" />
```

Authority is the authentication authority of the OAuth flow; you should use the above URL for the authority for the AAD based multitenant applications.

We will use the OWIN middleware for the authentication and OpenID protocol for the AAD authentication in our web application. In order to do this first, right-click on the project and add an OWIN Startup class, name it as Startup.cs (Figure 4-17).

Figure 4-17. *Adding OWIN Startup class*

Then install the following packages using the Package Manager Console using the below commands.

```
Install-Package Microsoft.Owin.Host.SystemWeb
Install-Package Microsoft.Owin.Security.OpenIdConnect
Install-Package Microsoft.Owin.Security.Cookies
```

AAD Authentication process is eligible only via HTTPS, and we have already set the reply URL to https://localhost:44300 in the Azure portal, so we should set this URL in the Visual Studio to run the application during the development.

Right-click on the project and go to Properties, click the Web tab (third option), and set the Project URL to the specified localhost URL (Figure 4-18).

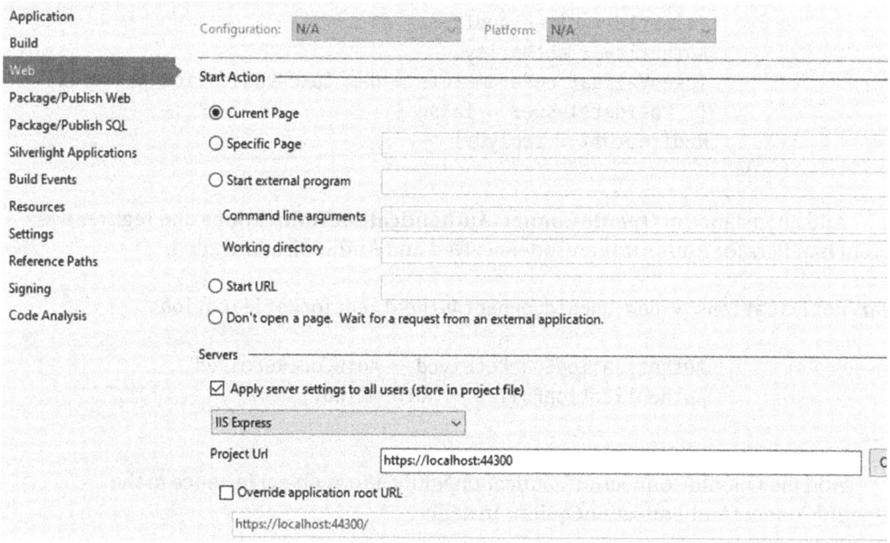

Figure 4-18. *Setting project URL in Visual Studio*

Now let's put some required code in the **Startup.cs**. First create three private variables in the Startup class to store the app setting values we stored in the web.config.

```
private string clientAppId = ConfigurationManager.AppSettings
["ClientAppId"].ToString();
private string authority = ConfigurationManager.AppSettings
["Authority"].ToString();
private string replyUrl = ConfigurationManager.AppSettings
["ReplyUrl"].ToString();
```

Then in the Configuration method enable the cookie based authentication and set the default authentication type to cookies.

```
app.UseCookieAuthentication(new CookieAuthenticationOptions()
{ CookieSecure = CookieSecureOption.Always });
app.SetDefaultSignInAsAuthenticationType(CookieAuthenticationDefaults.
AuthenticationType);
```

Then create an instance of **OpenIdConnectAuthenticationOptions** and set the properties below. Note that we set the ValidateIssuer to false, because in the multitenancy mode we can have custom validation of the tenants and handle the tenants using our custom logic.

Later in the code we will add some logic to check whether a tenant is registered; if not we will redirect the customer to a simulated payment page.

```
var options = new OpenIdConnectAuthenticationOptions
            {
                ClientId = clientAppId,
                Authority = authority,
                TokenValidationParameters = new TokenValidationParameters
                { ValidateIssuer = false },
                RedirectUri = replyUrl
            };
```

Add an instance of **OpenIdConnectAuthenticationNotifications** and register two event handlers for AuthorizationCodeReceived and AuthenticationFailed.

```
var notifications = new OpenIdConnectAuthenticationNotifications
            {
                AuthorizationCodeReceived = AuthCodeReceived,
                AuthenticationFailed = AuthFailed,
            };
```

Add the OpenIdConnectAuthenticationNotifications object instance to the OpenIdConnectAuthenticationOptions instance.

```
options.Notifications = notifications;
```

Finally add the **OpenIdConnectAuthenticationOptions** object to the OWIN app instance.

```
app.UseOpenIdConnectAuthentication(options);
```

Add the two event handlers we registered for the **OpenIdConnectAuthenticationNotifications** as two private methods.

```
public Task AuthCodeReceived(AuthorizationCodeReceivedNotification
notification)
        {
            return Task.FromResult(0);
        }
```

```
private Task AuthFailed(AuthenticationFailedNotification<OpenIdConnectMessa
ge, OpenIdConnectAuthenticationOptions> arg)
        {
            return Task.FromResult(0);
        }
```

Now we have done all the basic wire up and the required code to use AAD authentication in the application. At this stage the completed Startup class would have the following code.

```
public class Startup
    {
        private string clientAppId = ConfigurationManager.
        AppSettings["ClientAppId"].ToString();
        private string authority = ConfigurationManager.
        AppSettings["Authority"].ToString();
        private string replyUrl = ConfigurationManager.
        AppSettings["ReplyUrl"].ToString();

        public void Configuration(IAppBuilder app)
        {
            app.UseCookieAuthentication(new CookieAuthenticationOptions() {
            CookieSecure = CookieSecureOption.Always });
            app.SetDefaultSignInAsAuthenticationType(CookieAuthenticationDef
            aults.AuthenticationType);

            var options = new OpenIdConnectAuthenticationOptions
            {
                ClientId = clientAppId,
                Authority = authority,
                TokenValidationParameters = new TokenValidationParameters
                { ValidateIssuer = false },
                RedirectUri = replyUrl
            };

            var notifications = new OpenIdConnectAuthenticationNotifications
            {
                AuthorizationCodeReceived = AuthCodeReceived,
                AuthenticationFailed = AuthFailed,
            };

            options.Notifications = notifications;

            app.UseOpenIdConnectAuthentication(options);
        }

        public Task AuthCodeReceived(AuthorizationCodeReceivedNotification
        notification)
```

```
    {
        return Task.FromResult(0);
    }

    private Task AuthFailed(AuthenticationFailedNotification<OpenIdConne
    ctMessage, OpenIdConnectAuthenticationOptions> arg)
    {
        return Task.FromResult(0);
    }
}
```

Let's add some logic to the AuthCodeReceived method. In this method, we're sure that the user is a valid AAD user and we will have the Authentication code and the id_token.

Let's dissect the JWT based id_token, in this token we're interested in few claims for the DashDocs application. They are the following

1. oid – Object Identifier, the unique GUID from the respective AAD to identify the user. This will be used as the User ID in our database.

2. tid – Tenant Identifier, the unique GUID that identifies the AAD. Each AAD has a unique id and this will be used as the Customer ID in our database.

3. name – This is the name claim; this claim has the name of the user logged in.

In the AuthCodeReceived method, first we retrieve the mentioned claims from the id_token, and check whether the tid exists as a Customer ID in the Customers table in application database.

If the customer exists in the database, then we check whether the oid exists as a User in the Users table. If the User exists in the database, we simply sign in the user.

If the User doesn't exist for an existing Customer we add a new User record in the database and sign in the user.

```
public Task AuthCodeReceived(AuthorizationCodeReceivedNotification
notification)
        {
            var oid = Guid.Parse(notification.JwtSecurityToken.Claims.
            Single(c => c.Type == "oid").Value);
            var tid = Guid.Parse(notification.JwtSecurityToken.Claims.
            Single(c => c.Type == "tid").Value);
            var firstname = notification.JwtSecurityToken.Claims.Single(c =>
            c.Type == "name").Value;

            var context = new DashDocsContext();

            var customer = context.Customers.SingleOrDefault
            (c => c.Id == tid);
            if (customer != null)
```

```
    {
        var user = context.Users.SingleOrDefault(u => u.Id == oid &&
        u.CustomerId == tid);
        if (user == null)
        {
            // new user first sign-in
            user = new User
            {
                Id = oid,
                CustomerId = tid,
                FirstName = firstname
            };

            context.Users.Add(user);
            context.SaveChanges();
        }

        // though the application can access the claims from the
        returned
        // JWTToken, it's better to have custom claim properties as
        this eases up the usage.
        var applicationClaims = new AppClaims
        {
            CustomerId = tid,
            CustomerName = customer.Name,
            UserId = oid,
            DisplayName = user.FirstName
        };

        var claim = new Claim("ddcs", JsonConvert.SerializeObject(ap
        plicationClaims));
        notification.AuthenticationTicket.Identity.AddClaim(claim);
    }
    else
    {
        throw new UserLoggedInWithoutExistingCustomerException()
        {
            TenantId = tid,
            UserId = oid,
            FirstName = firstname
        };
    }
    return Task.FromResult(0);
}
```

Note that we create an instance of a custom class **AppClaims** and store the
information and persist that in the cookie using a key "ddcs" (key name can be any valid
string). The serilized values in the string will be deserialzed to the **AppClaims** instance
during the HTTP request and application gets the claims from the **AppClaims** instance.

If the Customer does not exist in the database, we throw an instance of
UserLoggedInWithoutExistingCustomerException and redirect the user to the
customer enrollment page from the AuthFailed method. If it's a different exception, we
simply ignore that in the AuthFailed method.

```
private Task AuthFailed(AuthenticationFailedNotification<OpenIdConnect
Message, OpenIdConnectAuthenticationOptions> arg)
        {
            var ex = arg.Exception as
            UserLoggedInWithoutExistingCustomerException;
            if (ex != null)
            {
                arg.OwinContext.Response.Redirect(

$"/customer/enroll?tid={ex.TenantId}&uid={ex.UserId}&fn={ex.FirstName}");
            }

            arg.HandleResponse();
            return Task.FromResult(0);
        }
```

Add the classes **AppClaims** and **UserLoggedInWithoutExistingCustomerException**
in the folders Helpers and Helpers/Exceptions respectively in the project tree.

AppClaims.cs

```
internal class AppClaims
    {
        public Guid CustomerId { get; set; }
        public string CustomerName { get; set; }
        public Guid UserId { get; set; }
        public string DisplayName { get; set; }
    }
```

UserLoggedInWithoutExistingCustomerException.cs

```
public class UserLoggedInWithoutExistingCustomerException : Exception
    {
        public Guid TenantId { get; set; }
        public Guid UserId { get; set; }
        public string FirstName { get; set; }
        public string LastName { get; set; }
    }
```

Let's complete the application with the proper wire-up to the controllers and
views. Each request from the client will contain the content of the cookies, including the
information we stored in the 'ddcs' property.

In order to make the value of this claim which is the JSON serialized **AppClaims** object available to all the controllers, let's create a base class **DashDocsControllerBase** inheriting **System.Web.Mvc.Controller.**

This base has a property **DashDocsClaims** and populates it during the controller initialize process. This property is accessible to all the other controllers since they derive from the **DashDocsControllerBase.**

DashDocsControllerBase.cs

```
public abstract class DashDocsControllerBase : Controller
    {
        protected override void Initialize(RequestContext requestContext)
        {
            base.Initialize(requestContext);

            if(User != null && User.Identity.IsAuthenticated)
            {
                var principal = (ClaimsPrincipal)User;
                var claim = principal.Claims.SingleOrDefault(c => c.Type ==
                "ddcs")?.Value;
                if (claim != null)
                {
                    DashDocsClaims = JsonConvert.DeserializeObject<AppClaim
                    s>(claim);
                }
                else
                {
                    throw new ApplicationException("Claims Null or
                    Unidentified : Authentication Exception");
                }
            }
        }

        internal AppClaims DashDocsClaims { get; private set; }
    }
```

Change the **HomeController** to derive from the **DashDocsControllerBase** and make the code changes from the hard-coded IDs to get the Customer ID and User ID from the **DashDocsClaims** property.

Do not forget to decorate the **HomeController** with the **Authorize** attribute as this is the key to fire up the authentication through OWIN.

HomeController.cs

```
[Authorize]
    public class HomeController : DashDocsControllerBase
    {
        public async Task<ActionResult> Index()
        {
            var customerId = DashDocsClaims.CustomerId;
```

```
            var dbContext = new DashDocsContext();
            var documents = from document in dbContext.Documents
                            join user in dbContext.Users on document.OwnerId
                            equals user.Id
                            where user.CustomerId == DashDocsClaims.
                            CustomerId
                            orderby document.CreatedOn descending
                            select document;

            return View(await documents.Include(d => d.Owner).Take(10).
            ToListAsync());
        }

        public async Task<ActionResult> Upload(HttpPostedFileBase document)
        {
            var blobStorageService = new BlobStorageService();
            var documentId = Guid.NewGuid();

            var path = await blobStorageService.UploadDocument
            Async(document, DashDocsClaims.CustomerId, documentId);

            var dbContext = new DashDocsContext();
            dbContext.Documents.Add(new Document
            {
                Id = documentId,
                DocumentName = Path.GetFileName(document.FileName).
                ToLower(),
                OwnerId = DashDocsClaims.UserId,
                CreatedOn = DateTime.UtcNow,
                BlobPath = path
            });
            await dbContext.SaveChangesAsync();

            return RedirectToAction("Index");
        }

        public async Task<FileResult> Download(Guid documentId)
        {
            var dbContext = new DashDocsContext();
            var document = await dbContext.Documents.SingleAsync
            (d => d.Id == documentId);

            var blobStorageService = new BlobStorageService();
            var content = await blobStorageService.DownloadDocumentAsync
            (documentId, DashDocsClaims.CustomerId);

content.Value.Position = 0;
```

```
        return File(content.Value, System.Net.Mime.MediaTypeNames.
        Application.Octet, content.Key);
    }

    [AllowAnonymous]
    public ActionResult About()
    {
        ViewBag.Message = "DashDocs Application";

        return View();
    }
}
```

Add a new Controller named **CustomerController.** We will have a single Action (Enroll) in this Controller for the new customer enrollment. The required values are passed to this Action via the query string. The Action adds the new Customer and the new User to the database and redirects the user to the Home Controller.

CustomerController.cs

```
[AllowAnonymous]
    public class CustomerController : Controller
    {
        public async Task<ActionResult> Enroll(Customer customer)
        {
            if (!Request.IsAuthenticated)
            {
                if (!string.IsNullOrWhiteSpace(customer.Name))
                {
                    customer.Id = Guid.Parse(Request.QueryString["tid"].
                    Trim());
                    var user = new User
                    {
                        Id = Guid.Parse(Request.QueryString["uid"].Trim()),
                        FirstName = Request.QueryString["fn"].Trim(),
                    };
                    customer.Users.Add(user);

                    var context = new DashDocsContext();
                    context.Customers.Add(customer);
                    await context.SaveChangesAsync();

                    return RedirectToAction("Index", "Home");
                }
                return View();
            }
            else
            {
                return RedirectToAction("Index", "Home");
```

```
            }
        }
    }
```

Add the view for the Enroll Action of the **CustomerController** with a text box to take customer name as the input.

Enroll.cshtml

```
@model DashDocs.Models.Customer

@{
    ViewBag.Title = "New Customer :)";
}

<div class="col-md-12 bg-blue">
    <h2>@ViewBag.Title</h2>
</div>

@using (Html.BeginForm())
{
    <div class="form-horizontal col-md-12 page-content">

        <h4>Welcome to DashDocs.</h4>
        <p>Thankyou for your interest in DashDocs. Please enter the name of
        your organization to get started!</p>
        <hr />

        @Html.ValidationSummary(true, "", new { @class = "text-danger" })
        <div class="form-group">
            @Html.LabelFor(model => model.Name, htmlAttributes: new
            { @class = "control-label col-md-2" })
            <div class="col-md-10">
                @Html.EditorFor(model => model.Name, new { htmlAttributes =
                new { @class = "form-control" } })
                @Html.ValidationMessageFor(model => model.Name, "", new { @
                class = "text-danger" })
            </div>
        </div>

        <div class="form-group">
            <div class="col-md-offset-2 col-md-10">
                <input type="submit" value="Create" class="btn btn-default" />
            </div>
        </div>
    </div>
}
```

Add another controller named **LogoutController** with a single Action that retrieves the current OWIN Context and signs out the user. Finally, it redirects to the Home, which, in turn, will trigger the AAD authentication flow.

LogoutController.cs

```
[Authorize]
    public class LogoutController : Controller
    {
        public ActionResult Index()
        {
            var ctx = Request.GetOwinContext();
            var authenticationManager = ctx.Authentication;

            authenticationManager.SignOut();
            return RedirectToAction("Index", "Home");
        }
    }
```

Finally, let's add simple modifications to the **_Layout.cshtml** to display the name of the logged-in user, and to show the Logout link.

_Layout.cshtml

```
<!DOCTYPE html>
<html>
<head>
    <meta charset="utf-8" />
    <meta name="viewport" content="width=device-width, initial-scale=1.0">
    <title>@ViewBag.Title - DashDocs</title>
    @Styles.Render("~/Content/css")
    @Scripts.Render("~/bundles/modernizr")
</head>
<body>
    <div class="navbar navbar-inverse navbar-fixed-top ">
        <div class="container-fluid ">
            <div class="navbar-header col-md-12">
                <button type="button" class="navbar-toggle" data-
                toggle="collapse" data-target=".navbar-collapse">
                    <span class="icon-bar"></span>
                    <span class="icon-bar"></span>
                    <span class="icon-bar"></span>
                </button>
                @Html.ActionLink("DashDocs", "Index", "Home", new
                { area = "" }, new { @class = "navbar-brand " })

                <div class="navbar-link pull-right padding-15">
                    @User.Identity.Name
                    @if (User.Identity.IsAuthenticated)
                    { <a href="/Logout">| Logout</a> }
                </div>

            </div>
        </div>
    </div>
```

```
<div class="container-fluid body-content no-padding">
    <div class="col-lg-1 col-md-2 col-sm-2 left-nav">
        <ul class="nav nav-pills nav-stacked">
            <li>@Html.ActionLink("Home", "Index", "Home")</li>
            <li>@Html.ActionLink("About", "About", "Home")</li>
        </ul>
    </div>
    <div class="col-lg-11 col-md-10 col-sm-10 no-padding">
        @RenderBody()

        <hr />
        <footer>
            <p class="footer">&copy; @DateTime.Now.Year -
            <a href="http://www.thuru.net" target="_blank">DashDocs</a></p>
        </footer>
    </div>

    </div>

@Scripts.Render("~/bundles/jquery")
@Scripts.Render("~/bundles/bootstrap")
@RenderSection("scripts", required: false)
</body>
</html>
```

Figure 4-19 shows the project structure after all of the required changes have been made.

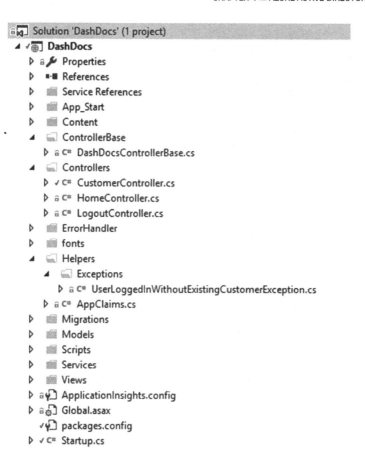

Figure 4-19. *Project structure*

We have completed all the required steps for the AAD integration with our MVC Application. Let's run the application in the development mode. Visual Studio will launch the application in the configured localhost URL (`https://localhost:44300`), and this will take the application to the AAD login page (Figure 4-20).

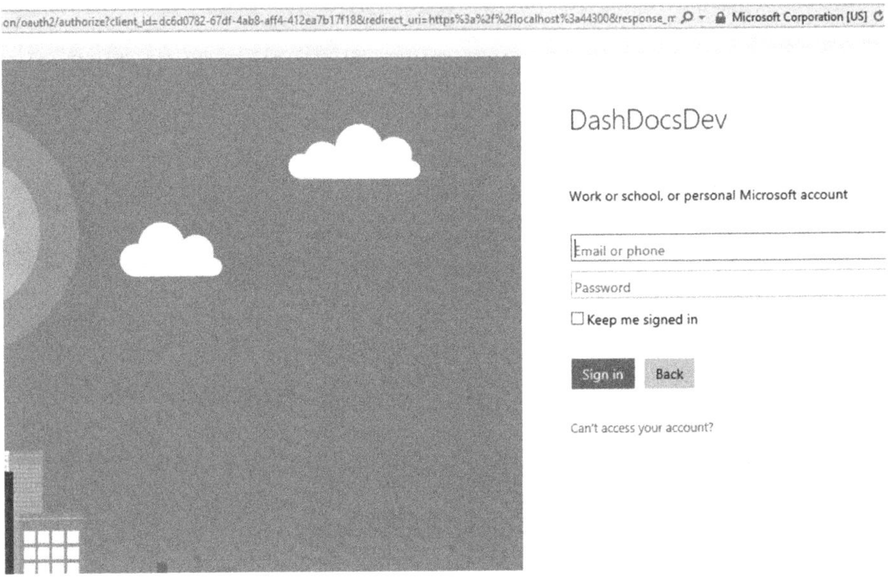

Figure 4-20. *Application landing on AAD login page*

Enter the credentials of the user – this user may be a Microsoft Account or a user in the current AAD (home tenant) or a user account in any other AAD. In this sample the credentials of the account administrator of the home tenant is used.

Since the Customer ID does not exist in the first attempt, the user will be taken to the customer enrollment page (Figure 4-21).

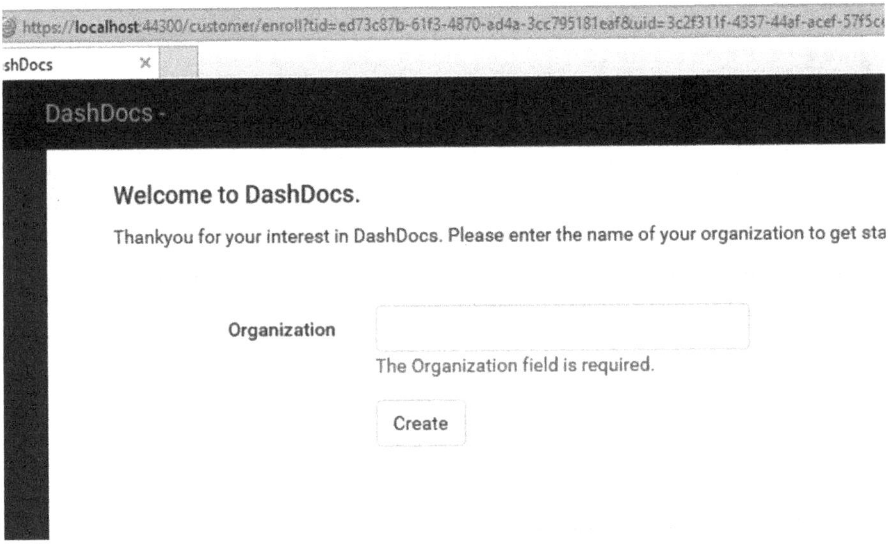

Figure 4-21. *Customer enrollment page*

Enter a name for the customer and click 'Create' to continue, also notice in the URL having the query string parameters tid, uid, and fn, which are the tenant Id – user Id and first name respectively.

This will save the new Customer and User record to the application database, and direct the user to the Home page (Figure 4-22), via the AAD authentication flow. This time the flow will succeed.

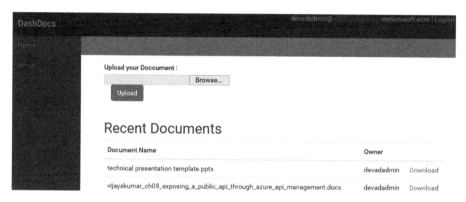

Figure 4-22. *Authenticated user in the home page*

Summary

This chapter covers the fundamentals of AAD and developing multitenant applications using AAD. As stated, multitenancy is not limited to this scope and it has many areas, especially in the data layers. DashDocs uses the shared database approach, but in some multitenanted applications we can go for a dedicated database for each tenant. Azure SQL Elastics pools can be used to manage the group databases that share the same schema for this purpose. Get the source code for this chapter from https://github.com/thuru/DashDocs/tree/master/DashDocs/Chapter%204.

Overall, this chapter gives us the crust of the AAD based multitenancy and application development overlook. DashDocs has grown even more at the end of this chapter, and the overall architecture of the DashDocs application is shown in Figure 4-23.

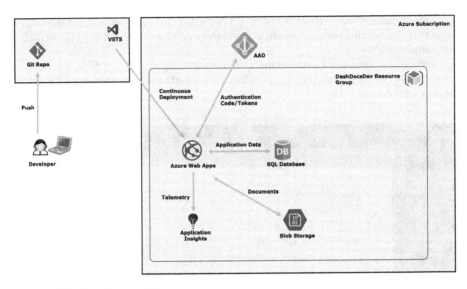

Figure 4-23. *DashDocs architecture overview*

CHAPTER 5

▓ ▓ ▓

Getting Started with Azure NoSQL Services

NoSQL persistence is popular and gaining accelerated dominance in the industry. The fundamental specialty of NoSQL persistence is that they can be scaled out with no or very few restrictions compared to the relations databases. NoSQL persistence also helps the modern application development with growing data in large volume, velocity, and velocity and veracity.

NoSQL based cloud service offerings are common, and most of the cloud based NoSQL services offer unlimited storage and unlimited scalability. NoSQL databases also support complex and unstructured data persistence and querying without much of the predefined schema constraint.

Like any modern cloud providers, Azure too has its own native NoSQL offerings and ported NoSQL offerings as well. Azure Table Storage is a key/value type NoSQL database that is very cheap compared to any other cloud based NoSQL offerings.

Azure Document DB is a document type NoSQL database. Document type NoSQL databases have gained more popularity than other types of NoSQL database due to the reduced development effort in data transformation in between services as almost all the document type NoSQL databases support JSON.

Azure Redis is a ported caching service on Azure, which is Redis infrastructure managed by Azure under different pricing and feature tiers. Redis is a very comprehensive caching technology that has inherent support for write-through persistence as well.

Azure Table Storage

Azure Table storage is part of the Azure storage services offerings. It is a key/value based NoSQL store. Table storage is a very cost effective yet high performing data persistence model. It has a high throughout in data inserts and querying. Providing high throughput in data inserts is one a core uniqueness of the Table storage. Due to this reason, Table storage is often used to save logs. Most of the Azure services also use Table storage for the logging purpose.

© Thurupathan Vijayakumar 2017
T. Vijayakumar, *Practical Azure Application Development*, DOI 10.1007/978-1-4842-2817-3_5

Creating a Table Storage

Let's create a Table storage to store the login logs of the DashDocs application. We will modify the application to persist the sign-in details in the Table storage.

Go to the portal and create a storage account as described in Chapter 2. But here we will **select the storage kind as General purpose one** (Figure 5-1).

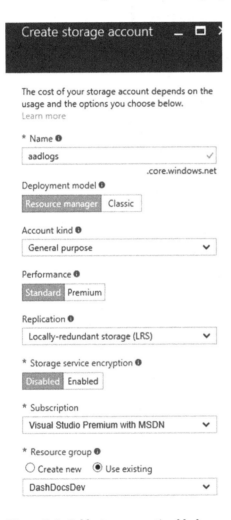

***Figure 5-1.** Table storage creation blade*

Navigate to the created general purpose storage account (Figure 5-2). There you can see the storage options like Blobs, Files, Queues, and Tables – these services are briefly described in Chapter 2.

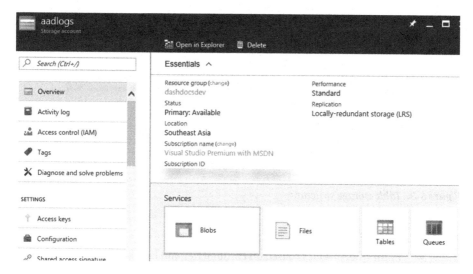

Figure 5-2. *General purpose storage account overview*

■ **Note**   General purpose storage accounts allow you to have all kinds of storage services, whereas the blob storage accounts are dedicated storage services for storing blobs. Blob storage accounts allows you to have different access tiers (hot/cold) based on the usage frequency of the data, but general purpose storage accounts do not have an option for the access tier, and it is considered equivalent to the hot access tier.

Click on the Tables, and you will see the blade with the existing tables. At this point the blade will be empty as we haven't created any tables yet.

Azure Table Storage Structure

Azure Table storage has tables as its base structure. A table has three in-built attributes, meaning the moment you create a table you already have these three fields defined. They are the following:

- **Partition Key** - Partition keys define the keys for the partition. Data in the Table storage are grouped in partitions.

- **Row Key** - Row key is a unique key to identify a row within a partition. Row keys cannot be duplicated inside a partition.

- **TimeStamp** - TimeStamp is used to track the last modified timestamp of the record.

99

The above structure (Figure 5-3) has two partitions and row keys are not duplicated inside a partition. **The combination of the partition key and the row key is unique across the table**.

Partition Key	Row Key	Timestamp	Custom Field1
1	a	2017-01-09T02:47:28.034Z	Timber Land
1	b	2017-02-09T02:47:28.034Z	Bean
2	a	2017-01-09T02:45:28.034Z	Blue Jar
2	b	2017-01-09T02:27:28.034Z	DKNY
2	c	2017-01-09T02:17:28.034Z	TIQRI

Figure 5-3. Table storage structure

Table storage supports four types of queries.

- **Point Query** - Query based on Partition Key and Row Key; retrieves single entity.

- **Range Query** - Query based on Partition Key and range of Row Keys; retrieves multiple entities.

- **Partition Scan** - Partition Key is used but Row Key is not known / not used in the in the query; other non-key fields might be used.

- **Table Scan** - Partition Key is not used in the query; other key fields might be used.

Table storage is a massively scalable high volume NoSQL database, and it has its limits defined in accordance with the Azure storage account. You can read more about the storage limits and quotas from this link: https://docs.microsoft.com/en-us/azure/storage/storage-scalability-targets

Table storage supports different data types like string, bool, DateTime, Guid, byte [], double, Int32, and long. These CLR types are mapped to the following OData types respectively: Edm.String, Edm.Boolean, Edm.DateTime, Edm.Guid, Edm.Binary, Edm. Double, Edm.Int32, and Edm.Int64. You can read more about data types from this link: https://docs.microsoft.com/en-us/rest/api/storageservices/fileservices/understanding-the-table-service-data-model

Programmatically Accessing Azure Table Storage

In order to access the Table storage, we use the same Azure storage NuGet packages we used to access the blob storage. The required packages are already available in the project as we used them in Chapter 2; in case if they are not referenced, install them using the following command.

```
Install-Package WindowsAzure.Storage
```

Next, we should set the storage account connection string in the web.config. This is also a similar step we performed in Chapter 2. In order to do this, we need to construct the storage account connection string from the storage account name and access key. Navigate to the storage and click the 'Keys' section and this will open the blade with the access keys (Figure 5-4).

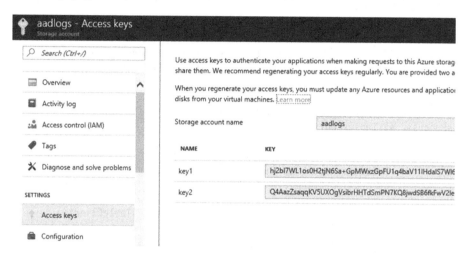

Figure 5-4. *Azure storage access keys*

Construct the connection string and store in in the connection strings section of the web.config as below.

```
<add name="LogStorage" connectionString="DefaultEndpointsProtocol=https;Acco
untName=<ACCOUNT NAME>;AccountKey=<ACCESS KEY>" />
```

Each individual data point of the Table storage is known as a Table entity. In our code, we need to create a Table Entity; in the .NET world, Table entities are simple POCOs that inherit the *TableEntity* class from the Azure storage library.

Add new a class named *SignInLog,* in the Models folder and inherit the *TableEntity* class.

SignInLogs.cs

```
public class SignInLogs : TableEntity
{
    public SignInLogs()
    {
    }

    public Guid UserId  { get; set; }
    public string IP { get; set; }
    public bool IsSuccess { get; set; }
    public string ExceptionMessage { get; set; }
}
```

101

TableEntity class has the Partition Key, Row Key, and TimeStamp properties that are now available in the *SignInLogs* class.

Insert Data to Azure Table Storage Using Azure Storage SDK

Let's add some code to persist data in the Table storage. Create a class named TableStorageService in the Services folder and add a method named CreateLog, which inserts the log record to the Table storage. **We will use the Tenant Id as the partition key and a new Guid for the Row key**.

```
public void CreateLog(Guid tenantId, Guid userId, string ip, bool
isSuccess, string exception)
        {
            var storageAccount = CloudStorageAccount.
            Parse(ConfigurationManager.ConnectionStrings["LogStorage"].
            ConnectionString);

            var tableClient = storageAccount.CreateCloudTableClient();

            var table = tableClient.GetTableReference($"DashDocs{DateTime.
            UtcNow.Year}");
            table.CreateIfNotExists();

            SignInLog entity = new SignInLog()
            {
                PartitionKey = tenantId.ToString(),
                RowKey = Guid.NewGuid().ToString(),
                UserId = userId,
                IP = ip,
                IsSuccess = isSuccess,
                ExceptionMessage = exception
            };

            TableOperation insertOperation = TableOperation.Insert(entity);
            table.ExecuteAsync(insertOperation);
        }
```

We create an instance of *CloudTableClient* and check whether the required table exists; if it does not exist, we create a new table. Note, for the table name, we append 'DashDocs' as a prefix to the year because **Table storage table names cannot begin with a numeric character**.

Then we create an instance of our *TableEntity* model (*SignInLogs*) and persist it using the insert *TableOperation*.

■ **Note** Defining and choosing the right keys for partitions and rows is an important aspect of designing solutions on Table storage because these keys highly influence the query performance.

It is better to define the partition keys and row keys in a way that we can calculate them in the application code.

For example, if you are to save user data in a table where email address is a unique property, it is better to create partitions with the first letter of the email and have the email address itself as a row key. This will help to distribute the data among different partitions while maintaining the uniqueness of the email address across the table.

Read this link to get more ideas about the table storage partitioning and row key allocation strategies: https://thuru.net/2015/12/30/design-an-online-forum-application-on-azure-table-storage/

We should call the method CreateLog from both the AuthCodeReceived and AuthFailed methods. The completed Startup.cs is shown below.
Startup.cs

```
public class Startup
    {
        private string clientAppId = ConfigurationManager.
        AppSettings["ClientAppId"].ToString();
        private string authority = ConfigurationManager.
        AppSettings["Authority"].ToString();
        private string replyUrl = ConfigurationManager.
        AppSettings["ReplyUrl"].ToString();

        public void Configuration(IAppBuilder app)
        {
            app.UseCookieAuthentication(new CookieAuthenticationOptions()
            { CookieSecure = CookieSecureOption.Always });

app.SetDefaultSignInAsAuthenticationType(CookieAuthenticationDefaults.
AuthenticationType);

            var options = new OpenIdConnectAuthenticationOptions
            {
                ClientId = clientAppId,
                Authority = authority,
                TokenValidationParameters = new TokenValidationParameters
                { ValidateIssuer = false },
                RedirectUri = replyUrl
            };
```

```
    var notifications = new OpenIdConnectAuthenticationNotifications
    {
        AuthorizationCodeReceived = AuthCodeReceived,
        AuthenticationFailed = AuthFailed,
    };

    options.Notifications = notifications;

    app.UseOpenIdConnectAuthentication(options);
}

public Task AuthCodeReceived(AuthorizationCodeReceivedNotification
notification)
{
    var oid = Guid.Parse(notification.JwtSecurityToken.Claims.
    Single(c => c.Type == "oid").Value);
    var tid = Guid.Parse(notification.JwtSecurityToken.Claims.
    Single(c => c.Type == "tid").Value);
    var firstname = notification.JwtSecurityToken.Claims.Single
    (c => c.Type == "name").Value;

    var context = new DashDocsContext();

    var customer = context.Customers.SingleOrDefault
    (c => c.Id == tid);
    if (customer != null)
    {
        var user = context.Users.SingleOrDefault(u => u.Id == oid &&
        u.CustomerId == tid);
        if (user == null)
        {
            // new user first sign-in
            user = new User
            {
                Id = oid,
                CustomerId = tid,
                FirstName = firstname
            };

            context.Users.Add(user);
            context.SaveChanges();
        }

        // though the application can access the claims from the
            returned
        // JWTToken, it's better to have custom claim properties as
            this eases up the usage.
        var applicationClaims = new AppClaims
```

```
        {
            CustomerId = tid,
            CustomerName = customer.Name,
            UserId = oid,
            DisplayName = user.FirstName + user.LastName
        };

        var claim = new Claim("ddcs", JsonConvert.SerializeObject(ap
        plicationClaims));

        notification.AuthenticationTicket.Identity.AddClaim(claim);

        var tableStorageService = new TableStorageService();
        tableStorageService.CreateLog(tid, oid, notification.
        Request.RemoteIpAddress, true, null);
    }
    else
    {
        throw new UserLoggedInWithoutExistingCustomerException()
        {
            TenantId = tid,
            UserId = oid,
            FirstName = firstname
        };
    }
    return Task.FromResult(0);
}

private Task AuthFailed(AuthenticationFailedNotification<OpenIdConne
ctMessage, OpenIdConnectAuthenticationOptions> arg)
{
    var ex = arg.Exception as
    UserLoggedInWithoutExistingCustomerException;
    if (ex != null)
    {
        arg.OwinContext.Response.Redirect(

$"/customer/enroll?tid={ex.TenantId}&uid={ex.UserId}&fn={ex.FirstName}");

        var tableStorageService = new TableStorageService();
        tableStorageService.CreateLog(ex.TenantId, ex.UserId, arg.
        Request.RemoteIpAddress, false, "User Logged In Without
        Existing Customer");
    }

    arg.HandleResponse();
    return Task.FromResult(0);
    }
}
```

Retrieve Data from Azure Table Storage Using Azure Storage SDK

In the context of application logging, we usually wouldn't have a user interface to see the logs. We use the existing tools or custom-developed tools to explore the data. Microsoft Azure Storage Explorer is a handy tool in exploring Azure Storage.

In order to demonstrate the querying aspect of the Table storage, let's have a method named GetLogsForTenant in the TableStorageService class. Azure Storage SDK provides methods that go hand in hand with the LINQ queries, thus enabling developers to use similar syntax in querying the table storage.

```
public List<SignInLogs> GetLogsForTenant(int year, string tenantId, bool
status)
        {
            var storageAccount = CloudStorageAccount.
            Parse(ConfigurationManager.ConnectionStrings["LogStorage"].
            ConnectionString);

            var tableClient = storageAccount.CreateCloudTableClient();
            var table = tableClient.GetTableReference($"DashDocs{year}");

            var query = from log in table.CreateQuery<SignInLogs>()
                        where log.PartitionKey == tenantId && log.IsSuccess
                        == status
                        select log;

            return query.ToList();
        }
```

The above query is a partition scan where the partition key is used along with another non-row key field (status). Table storage scans within the partition for the specified records.

Note Azure Table storage supports many operations and there are numerous use cases; the above section covers a basic getting started scenario of the Table storage with simple insert and querying operations.

Azure Document DB

Azure Document DB is a document type NoSQL database service in Azure. It is a JSON based, popular service among modern web and mobile applications. Document DB has an SQL-like syntax for direct querying and supports MongoDB API queries as well, which makes Document DB a friendly NoSQL option in Azure.

In the DashDocs application, we will introduce a feature so that users can comment on the documents, and we will use Azure Document DB to store these comments.

Azure Document DB Structure

Azure Document DB service is packaged under the Document DB account. Document has Document DB databases that are logical containers with one or more collections and users. Collections are the billable persistence containers for the documents. Collections also contain stored procedures, user-defined functions, and triggers. Figure 5-5 shows the resource structure of the Document DB.

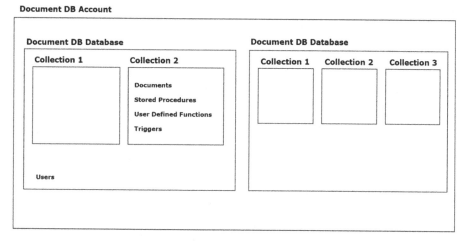

Figure 5-5. Document DB resource structure

Creating Azure Document DB

Go to Azure portal and search for Document DB (Figure 5-6) and let's create a Document DB account. Choose this option to create a new Document DB account. This will open the Document DB account creation blade.

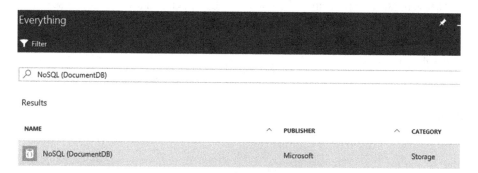

Figure 5-6. Choosing Document DB in the portal to create

107

In the Document DB account creation blade (Figure 5-7) enter a name for the Document DB account; select the Document DB as the NoSQL API; and create the account by choosing the subscription, resource group, and the location.

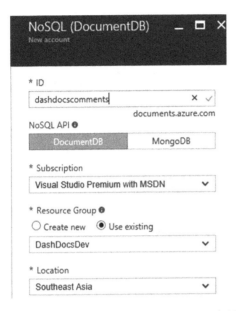

Figure 5-7. Document DB account creation blade

After creating the Document DB account, we should create a Document DB database and a collection inside the database to store the comments. In the simplest form, we will use a single collection to store all the comments from all the customers. But in real application development, these decisions are influenced by many other factors like performance, data separation, etc.

■ **Note**   Choosing the collections and planning the data persistence is a critical step in the application design using Document DB. Choose the collections and documents with self-contained information that will reduce the lookups with other collections and documents. But also, be mindful about frequent updates to a document and, as a good practice, try to reduce the updates.

Let's create the Document DB collection to store the comments. Navigate to the Document DB account (Figure 5-8).

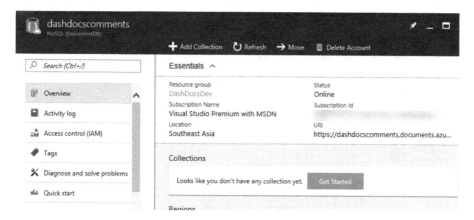

Figure 5-8. Document DB account overview blade

Click the 'Add Collection' button, and it will open the collection creation blade (Figure 5-9). There are several parameters you have to choose when creating a collection.

- **Name** – Name of the collection.

- **Storage Capacity** – This is available under three different options: 10GB, 250GB, and Custom. Custom capacity requires you to contact the Azure support and provision the resources. In theory, there's no storage limit for Document DB, but you can always request more, when required, by contacting Azure support.

- **Throughput Capacity** – This is a very important parameter. Throughput is measured in Request Unit (RU) per second. Different storage capacities provide different ranges of RU/s. 10GB storage provides throughput from 400 RU/s to 10,000 RU/s, 250GB storage provides throughput from 2500 RU/s to 25,0000 RU/s. Like storage throughput, capacity can be configured to custom levels via support requests.

- **Partition Key** – This is not mandatory in the 10GB storage capacity but a mandatory property in the 250GB storage capacity. This automatically partitions the data across multiple servers for scalability. You can provide the name/path of your JSON attribute in your document as a partition key and Document DB will automatically manage the partitioning for you.

- **Database** – The Document DB database; either you can create a new database or select an existing one. Since we do not have a database at this point, you will need to create a new one.

109

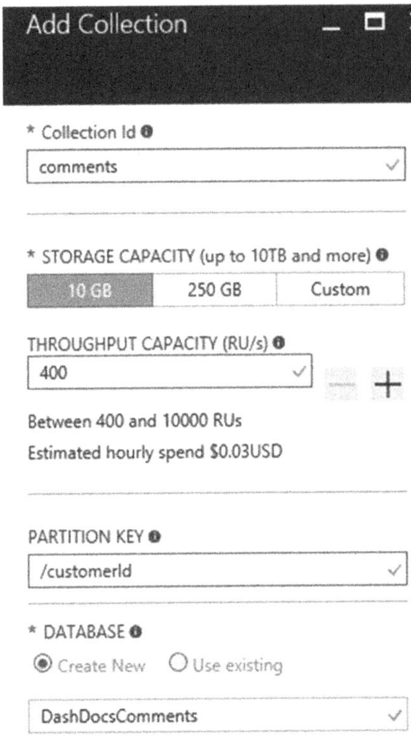

Figure 5-9. *Collection creation blade*

In our application, we will use the *customerId* attribute as the partition key in order to distribute the comments from different customers to different servers.

▦ **Note**   Document DB Request Unit (RU) corresponds to the throughput of a read of 1KB document. 100 RU/s throughput means we can have the throughput of 100KB/second read.

Document DB RU calculator is a handy tool to determine the required RUs for the application (https://www.documentdb.com/capacityplanner). You can upload your sample documents in different states, specify the number of estimated reads and writes, and get an estimated total of RUs and the required storage.

When you exceed the throughput limit, **Document DB will respond with the HTTP status code of 429 with the message and retry time in milliseconds**. Document DB .NET client SDK has an in-built mechanism to handle this and retry without any custom logic.

Document DB Consistency Levels

Typical NoSQL databases offer two consistency levels – strong and eventual consistency. Document DB offers two additional consistency levels, session and bounded staleness.

- Strong – Ensures the most recent writes are read. Document DB accounts that are configured with the strong consistency cannot associate more than one Azure region, meaning global distribution is not possible.

- Bounded staleness – Ensures that reads may lag the writes by particular number of versions or a specified time interval. So, when choosing this option, we can specify the staleness either by the number of versions or by the time interval. This option is best suited when we require near strong consistency and globally distributed storage.

- Session – This is scoped to a client session. Ensures monotonic reads, monotonic writes, and ensures read your own writes. Supports global distribution. This is the default consistency level in Document DB.

- Eventual – Ensures that in the absence of any further writes, the reads will be consistent with the last write. Weakest consistency but offers lowest latency for both writes and reads.

With the two additional consistency models Document DB has four consistency models where the Bounded Staleness is closer to the Strong consistency and Session is closer to the Eventual consistency.

You can read more about Document DB consistency levels from this link: `https://docs.microsoft.com/en-us/azure/documentdb/documentdb-consistency-levels`

Programmatically Access Azure Document DB with SDK

Let's begin the development with Document DB. We should acquire the connection settings of the Document DB. Navigate to the Document DB account we created, and click on 'Keys'. This will open the blade (Figure 5-10) with the respective access keys and the connection strings.

Copy the URI and the primary key of the Document DB account and place it in the app settings of the web.config.

```
<add key="DocumentDb:Uri" value="<URI>"/>
<add key="DocumentDb:Key" value="<ACCESS KEY>"></add>
```

Install the following NuGet package.

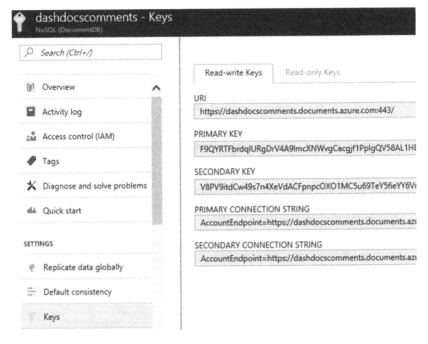

Figure 5-10. *Document DB connection strings*

Install-Package Microsoft.Azure.DocumentDB

First, let's create the required document model class. Create a class named Comment in the Models folder. In the Comment.cs add another class CommentDateTime. This class is used to store the DateTime as an epoch value, since Document DB does not support DateTime type.

Epoch is a value that is the difference of the current timestamp from a specified timestamp value in seconds.

Comment.cs

```
public class Comment
    {
        [JsonProperty(PropertyName = "id")]
        public string Id { get; set; }
        [JsonProperty(PropertyName = "documentId")]
        public Guid DocuemtnId { get; set; }
        [JsonProperty(PropertyName = "customerId")]
        public Guid CustomerId { get; set; }
        [JsonProperty(PropertyName = "content")]
        public string Content { get; set; }
        [JsonProperty(PropertyName = "author")]
        public string Author { get; set; }
        [JsonProperty(PropertyName = "commentDateTime")]
        public CommentDateTime CommentDateTime { get; set; }
    }
```

```
public class CommentDateTime
{
    [JsonProperty(PropertyName = "dateStamp")]
    public DateTime DateStamp { get; set; }
    [JsonProperty(PropertyName = "epoch")]
    public int Epoch { get; set; }
}
```

Note that each document in the Document DB should have an id property that should be a unique string within the collection.

Create a class named DocumentDbService in the Services folder. We need two methods in this class, one for inserting the comment to the Document DB collection and the other one for retrieving the comments for the specified document. We also have a private method for the epoch calculation. Note that this private method can be implemented as a JSONConverter as well.

DocumentDbService.cs

```
public class DocumentDbService
{
    private static readonly DocumentClient _documentClient;

    private static readonly string _database = "DashDocsComments";
    private static readonly string _collection = "comments";

    static DocumentDbService()
    {
        var uri = ConfigurationManager.AppSettings["DocumentDb:Uri"].
        ToString();
        var key = ConfigurationManager.AppSettings["DocumentDb:Key"].
        ToString();
        _documentClient = new DocumentClient(new Uri(uri), key);
    }

    public async Task CreateCommentAsync(Comment comment)
    {
        comment.CommentDateTime = GetCommentDateTime();
        await _documentClient.CreateDocumentAsync(UriFactory.
        CreateDocumentCollectionUri(_database, _collection), comment);
    }

    public async Task<List<Comment>> GetCommentsAsync(Guid documentId,
    Guid customerId)
    {
        var query = _documentClient.CreateDocumentQuery<Comment>(UriFact
        ory.CreateDocumentCollectionUri(_database, _collection))
```

```
            .Where(c => c.DocuemtnId == documentId && c.CustomerId ==
            customerId).AsDocumentQuery();

    var comments = new List<Comment>();
    while (query.HasMoreResults)
    {
        comments.AddRange(await query.ExecuteNextAsync<Comment>());
    }
    return comments;
}

private CommentDateTime GetCommentDateTime()
{
    var datetime = DateTime.UtcNow;
    return new CommentDateTime
    {
        DateStamp = datetime,
        Epoch = (int)((datetime - new DateTime(1987, 8, 8)).
        TotalSeconds)
    };
}
}
```

Notice that the Document DB client is instantiated in the static constructor; this is a general practice in working with Document DB SDK. We do not instantiate the client on each request.

Let's complete this by adding a new controller and the corresponding view. Add a new controller named DocumentController.

DocumentControll.cs

```
[Authorize]
    public class DocumentController : DashDocsControllerBase
    {
        public async Task<ActionResult> Index()
        {
            Guid documentId = Guid.Empty;

            if (Request.QueryString["documentId"] != null && Guid.
            TryParse(Request.QueryString["documentId"], out documentId))
            {
                var dbContext = new DashDocsContext();
                var document = dbContext.Documents.Single(d => d.Id ==
                documentId);

                var docucmentDbContext = new DocumentDbService();
                var comments = await docucmentDbContext.
                GetCommentsAsync(documentId, DashDocsClaims.CustomerId);
```

```
                var result = new KeyValuePair<Document,
                List<Comment>>(document, comments);
                return View(result);
            }
            else
            {
                return RedirectToAction("Index", "Home");
            }
        }

        [HttpPost]
        public async Task<ActionResult> Comment(string content, Guid
        documentId)
        {
            var comment = new Comment
            {
                Content = content,
                Author = DashDocsClaims.DisplayName,
                CustomerId = DashDocsClaims.CustomerId,
                DocuemtnId = documentId,
                Id = Guid.NewGuid().ToString()
            };
            var docucmentDbContext = new DocumentDbService();
            await docucmentDbContext.CreateCommentAsync(comment);

            return RedirectToAction("Index", new { documentId = documentId
});
        }
    }
```

DocumentController has a single view
Document/Index.cshtml

```
@model KeyValuePair<DashDocs.Models.Document, List<DashDocs.Models.Comment>>

@{
    ViewBag.Title = "Index";
}

<div class="col-md-12 bg-blue">
    <h2>@Model.Key.DocumentName</h2>
</div>

<div class="col-md-12 page-content">
    @using (Html.BeginForm("Comment", "Document", FormMethod.Post))
    {
        <div class="form-inline padding-top-25">
            <div class="form-group">
```

```
                    <label >Comment</label><br />
                    <textarea type="text" class="form-control" name="content"
                    cols="40"></textarea>
                    <input type="hidden" value="@Model.Key.Id"
                    name="documentId" />
                    <button type="submit" value="Post" class="btn btn-
                    primary">Post</button>
               </div>
          </div>
     }

     <div id="comments" class="padding-top-25">
          @foreach (var item in Model.Value)
          {                                    •
               <div id="comment">
                    <span id="content">@item.Content</span>
                    <span class="badge"><span id="author">by @item.Author</
                    span></span>
                    <hr/>
               </div>
          }
     </div>
</div>
```

In order to navigate to the Document/Index.cshtml we should add a link named 'Details' in the Home/Index.cshtml table.

Home/Index.cshtml

```
@model IEnumerable<DashDocs.Models.Document>

<div class="col-md-12 bg-blue">
    @{
         ViewBag.Title = "DashDocs";
    }

</div>
    <div class="col-md-12 page-content">
        <div class="col-md-12 no-padding">
            @using (Html.BeginForm("Upload", "Home", FormMethod.Post, new {
            enctype = "multipart/form-data" }))
            {
                <div class="form-group padding-top-25">
                        <label class="control-label ">Upload your Doccument
                        : </label>
                    <div class="col-md-12 no-padding">
                        <input type="file" name="document" id="document" />
                    </div>
                </div>
```

```
            <div class="form-group">
                <div class="col-md-10 padding-tb-15">
                    <input type="submit" value="Upload" class="btn btn-
                    primary" />
                </div>
            </div>
        }
    </div>

    <div class="col-md-12 div-table">
        <h2>Recent Documents</h2>
        <table class="table table-hover">
            <tr>
                <th>
                    Document Name
                </th>
                <th>
                    Owner
                </th>
                <th></th>
            </tr>
            <tbody>
                @foreach (var item in Model)
                {
                    <tr>
                        <td>
                            @Html.DisplayFor(modelItem => item.
                            DocumentName)
                        </td>
                        <td>
                            @Html.DisplayFor(modelItem => item.Owner.
                            FirstName)
                        </td>
                        <td>
                            @Html.ActionLink("Details", "Index",
                            "Document", new { documentId = item.Id },
                            new { }) |
                            @Html.ActionLink("Download", "Download", new
                            { documentId = item.Id })

                        </td>
                    </tr>
                }
            </tbody>
        </table>

    </div>
</div>
```

117

Run the application and now the Home/Index.cshtml would look similar to Figure 5-11 with the additional link named 'Details' in each row.

Upload your Doccument :

Choose File   No file chosen

Upload

Recent Documents

Document Name	Owner	
technology orchestration guide for the businesses.docx	devadadmin	Details | Download
architecture overview.docx	devadadmin	Details | Download

© 2017 - DashDocs

***Figure 5-11.** New home page grid view*

Clicking on the 'Details' will take you to the Document/Index.cshtml. There you can make the comments and they will be saved in the Document DB, and existing comments will be visible under the document (Figure 5-12).

technology orchestration guide for the businesses.docx

Comment

Post

Images should be labeled (by devadadminadmin)

this is version 1.1, require some improvements. (by devadadminadmin)

© 2017 - DashDocs

***Figure 5-12.** Document comments view*

Navigate to the Document DB section of in the Azure portal and click on the 'Query Explorer' (Figure 5-13). Here you can use the SQL-like syntax and query the Document DB. This syntax can also be used in the application as well.

Figure 5-13. *Document DB Query Explorer*

Note that there are some system properties in each document. These system properties begin with _ and are generated by the system.

- _rid – This is the unique and hierarchical identifier of the resource. The abbreviation for the resource identifier.

- _etag – ETag value for the optimistic concurrency.

- _ts – Last updated timestamp of the resource.

- _self – Unique addressable URI of the resource. Each document has a URI in Document DB.

■ **Note** Document DB supports many operations and there are numerous use cases; the above section covers a basic getting started scenario of the Document DB with simple insert and querying operations.

Redis

Redis is a cache with many advanced features that make Redis the leading caching solution in many industries. Sometimes Redis is categorized under the NoSQL solutions as well. Redis is available as a service in Azure.

Compared to mere key/value based caching techniques, Redis has specially defined data types and operations. In this section let's use Redis to store the recent documents we display in the Home page.

Setting Up Redis on Azure

Navigate to the Azure portal and select Search for Redis, and choose the Redis option from Microsoft to create it (Figure 5-14).

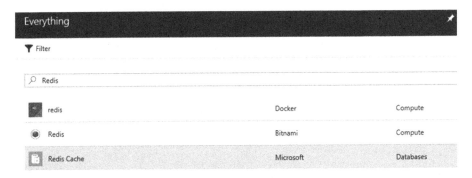

Figure 5-14. *Choosing Redis as a service in Azure*

Note that Redis is available in other flavors as well, especially in VMs and containers. Also, there are other third-party providers of Redis through Azure Marketplace offerings. Select the option shown in Figure 5-14 and this will open the Redis as a service creation blade (Figure 5-15).

Enter the DNS name for the Redis service and choose the other known options. Under the pricing tier you will see different options. For this purpose, we have selected the Standard tier and because of that the three premium tier options remain disabled.

Premium tier offers Redis clusters as we specify the number of shards. Premium tier also offers the data persistence so that we can configure a storage account and the backup frequency of the data persistence. Virtual Network support is also available in the premium tier.

After filling in the required information for the Standard tier, click 'Create' to begin the deployment.

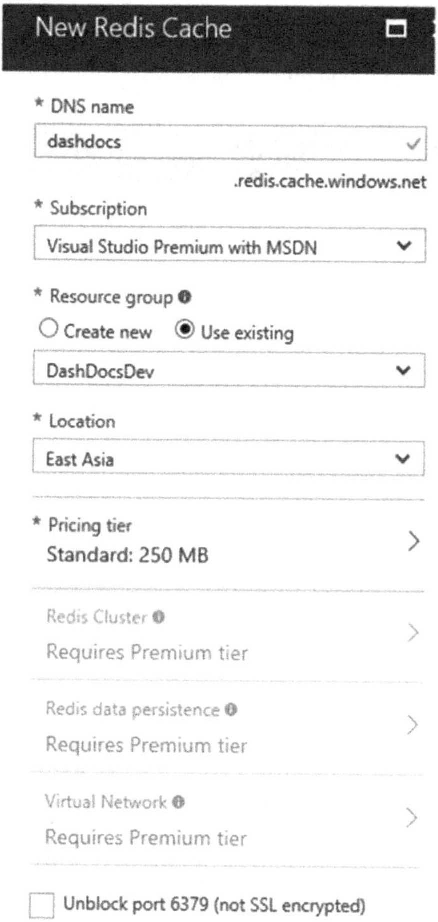

New Redis Cache ◻

* DNS name

dashdocs   ✓

.redis.cache.windows.net

* Subscription

Visual Studio Premium with MSDN   ⌄

* Resource group ❶

○ Create new   ◉ Use existing

DashDocsDev   ⌄

* Location

East Asia   ⌄

* Pricing tier   >
Standard: 250 MB

Redis Cluster ❶   >
Requires Premium tier

Redis data persistence ❶   >
Requires Premium tier

Virtual Network ❶   >
Requires Premium tier

☐ Unblock port 6379 (not SSL encrypted)

Figure 5-15. *Redis service creation blade*

Now let's begin the development; we will use Redis to store the 10 recent documents of each customer. We will use a Redis List to store recent documents against the customer Id as the key. This list will provide the data required to be displayed in the Home page.

Accessing Redis Service on Azure through SDK

We will use the StackExchange.Redis NuGet package. Redis has various drivers, and StackExchange.Redis is a popular one. Install the driver using the following command.

```
Install-Package StackExchange.Redis
```

121

In order to begin the development, we need the connection parameters of our Redis instance, like any other Redis service – navigate to the Redis instance we created and click on the 'Access keys'. This will open the Redis service connection string blade (Figure 5-16).

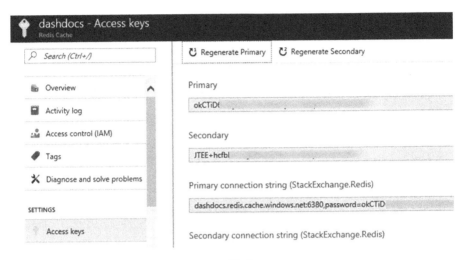

Figure 5-16. *Redis service connection string blade*

Copy one of the available connection strings and place it in the web.config connection strings section.

```
<add name="Redis" connectionString="<CONNECTION STRING>"/>
```

Since the purpose of this cache is to store the recent documents and display them in the home page, we will create a simple view model. Create a folder named ViewModels in the project and add a DocumentViewModel class.

DocumentViewModel.cs

```
public class DocumentViewModel
    {
        public Guid DocumentId { get; set; }
        public string DocumentName { get; set; }
        public string Owner { get; set; }
        public DateTime CreatedOn { get; set; }
    }
```

Create a class named RedisService in the Services folder. This class should have two methods, one for updating the Redis list when a new document is uploaded by a user, and the next method is to retrieve the recent documents from the cache for the given customer Id.

RedisService.cs

```csharp
public class RedisService
    {
        private static Lazy<ConnectionMultiplexer> _lazyConnection;

        private static ConnectionMultiplexer cacheConnection
        {
            get
            {
                return _lazyConnection.Value;
            }
        }

        static RedisService()
        {
            _lazyConnection = new Lazy<ConnectionMultiplexer>(() =>
            {
                return ConnectionMultiplexer.Connect(ConfigurationManager.
                ConnectionStrings["Redis"].ConnectionString);
            });
        }

        private readonly IDatabase _cache;

        public RedisService()
        {
            _cache = cacheConnection.GetDatabase();
        }

        public async Task UpdateDocumentCacheAsync(Guid customerId,
        DocumentViewModel document)
        {
            var customerKey = customerId.ToString().ToString();
            var documentJson = JsonConvert.SerializeObject(document);

            // this will insert the element at the head of the list.
            // if the list does not exist for the specified key, a new empty
            list will be created
            await _cache.ListLeftPushAsync(customerKey, documentJson);

            // here we do the trimming of the list - A Redis operation
            // 0 - 9 elements to keep from the head : keeps 10 documents
            _cache.ListTrimAsync(customerKey, 0, 9, CommandFlags.
            FireAndForget);
        }
        public async Task<List<DocumentViewModel>> GetRecentDocumentsForCust
        omerAsync(Guid customerId)
        {
            var customerKey = customerId.ToString().ToString();
```

123

```
            // get all the elements from the list starting from head zero
            based index to -1 means the last element
            var documentJsons = await _cache.ListRangeAsync
            (customerKey, 0, -1, CommandFlags.None);

            var documents = new List<DocumentViewModel>();
            foreach (var json in documentJsons)
            {
                documents.Add(JsonConvert.DeserializeObject<DocumentViewMod
                el>(json));
            }

            return documents;
        }
    }
```

Notice that we have used a Lazy static property to keep the **ConnectionMultiplexer** object. StackExchange.Redis uses connection multiplexing to manage connections to the Redis, and this shares the connections among different requests and is considered a general practice in StackExchange.Redis development.

In the UpdateDocumentAsync we create a Redis list and push the elements to the head of the list; also we trim the list to keep the 10 items. Since trimming is an inside operation for the document update, we use the FireAndForget command flag.

In the GetRecentDocumentsForCustomerAsync method we retrieve all the items of the list (maximum can be 10) and populate the Document collection and return it.

We need to update the HomeController actions to use the RedisService. First, we need to update the Upload action, and when a document is uploaded to the blob storage, we do the database record insertion and update the cache.

```
public async Task<ActionResult> Upload(HttpPostedFileBase document)
        {
            var blobStorageService = new BlobStorageService();
            var documentId = Guid.NewGuid();

            var path = await blobStorageService.UploadDocumentAsync(document,
            DashDocsClaims.CustomerId, documentId);

            var dbContext = new DashDocsContext();

            var documentModel = new Document
            {
                Id = documentId,
                DocumentName = Path.GetFileName(document.FileName).
                ToLower(),
                OwnerId = DashDocsClaims.UserId,
                CreatedOn = DateTime.UtcNow,
                BlobPath = path
            };
```

```
dbContext.Documents.Add(documentModel);
await dbContext.SaveChangesAsync();

var doc = new DocumentViewModel
{
    DocumentId = documentModel.Id,
    Owner = DashDocsClaims.DisplayName,
    CreatedOn = documentModel.CreatedOn,
    DocumentName = documentModel.DocumentName,
};

var redisService = new RedisService();
await redisService.UpdateDocumentCacheAsync(DashDocsClaims.
CustomerId, doc);

return RedirectToAction("Index");
}
```

Then, we need to change the Index action of the HomeController, to retrieve the recent documents from the cache.

```
public async Task<ActionResult> Index()
    {
        var redisService = new RedisService();
        var collection = await redisService.GetRecentDocumentsForCustome
        rAsync(DashDocsClaims.CustomerId);

        return View(collection);
    }
```

Finally let's modify the Home/Index.cshtml to accommodate the new changes with the view model class.

Home/Index.cshtml

```
@model IEnumerable<DashDocs.ViewModels.DocumentViewModel>

<div class="col-md-12 bg-blue">
    @{
        ViewBag.Title = "DashDocs";
    }

</div>
    <div class="col-md-12 page-content">
        <div class="col-md-12 no-padding">
            @using (Html.BeginForm("Upload", "Home", FormMethod.Post, new
            { enctype = "multipart/form-data" }))
            {
                <div class="form-group padding-top-25">
```

```
                    <label class="control-label ">Upload your Doccument
                    : </label>
                <div class="col-md-12 no-padding">
                    <input type="file" name="document" id="document" />
                </div>
            </div>

            <div class="form-group">
                <div class="col-md-10 padding-tb-15">
                    <input type="submit" value="Upload" class="btn
                    btn-primary" />
                </div>
            </div>
    }
</div>

<div class="col-md-12 div-table">
    <h2>Recent Documents</h2>
    <table class="table table-hover">
        <tr>
            <th>
                Document Name
            </th>
            <th>
                Owner
            </th>
            <th>
                Created On
            </th>
            <th></th>
        </tr>
        <tbody>
            @foreach (var item in Model)
            {
                <tr>
                    <td>
                        @Html.DisplayFor(modelItem => item.
                        DocumentName)
                    </td>
                    <td>
                        @Html.DisplayFor(modelItem => item.Owner)
                    </td>
                    <td>
                        @Html.DisplayFor(modelItem => item.
                        CreatedOn)
                    </td>
                    <td>
                        @Html.ActionLink("Details", "Index",
                        "Document", new { documentId = item.
                        DocumentId }, new { }) |
```

```
                    @Html.ActionLink("Download", "Download", new
                    { documentId = item.DocumentId })

                </td>
            </tr>
        }
        </tbody>
    </table>

    </div>
</div>
```

Run the Application and you will see the list of documents on the home page (Figure 5-17). Though you will not see any changes in the interface, try uploading more than 10 documents and you will notice that you see only the most recent 10 documents in the grid. You can check the records against the database for all the documents.

Upload your Document :

Choose File No file chosen

Upload

Recent Documents

Document Name	Owner	Created On	
training need analysis.docx	Thuru	24-Feb-17 7:04:37 AM	Details	Download
architecture overview.docx	Thuru	24-Feb-17 7:04:27 AM	Details	Download
structure businesscv- v5.docx	Thuru	24-Feb-17 7:04:14 AM	Details	Download

Figure 5-17. *Application with Redis integration*

Monitoring Redis Using Azure Portal

After uploading a few documents, navigate to the Redis service and in the overview section, click the 'Console' (Figure 5-18).

Figure 5-18. *Console option in the overview blade*

This will open the Redis console in the Azure portal (Figure 5-19).

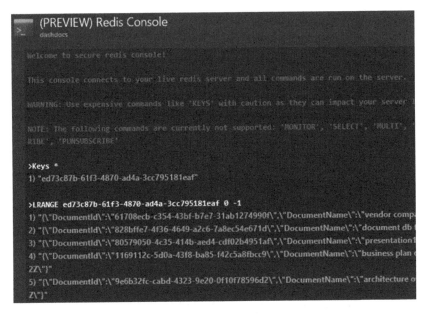

Figure 5-19. *Redis command line in Azure portal*

Execute the Redis command Keys *, and this will list all the keys in the Redis space. DO NOT exercise this in a production environment as this will increase the server load.

Then execute the LRANGE command with the parameters 0 and -1, which ensures that you can retrieve all the elements of the list for the specified key.

After completing all the required code and changes, DashDocs project has gotten more additions of files. Figure 5-20 shows the current structure of the project.

Figure 5-20. *Project structure*

Summary

We have integrated three different types of NoSQL services from Azure and used them for different purposes. The information provided in this chapter is sufficient enough to get started with those services, but each of them is big enough that you can dig deeper into them with various use cases and application design paradigms. Get the source code for this chapter from `https://github.com/thuru/DashDocs/tree/master/DashDocs/Chapter%205`.

The overall architecture of the DashDocs application is shown in Figure 5-21.

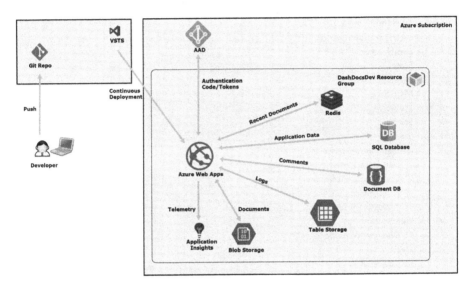

Figure 5-21. *DashDocs application overview*

CHAPTER 6

▓ ▓ ▓

Security and Data Protection

Security and data protection are one of the major concerns in cloud development. This is a huge topic that spans many aspects like authentication, data protection, privacy, encryption, network security, monitoring, threat detection, and much more.

In Chapter 4, we covered AAD as a cloud-based authentication service that can act as an extension of the on-premises AD as well. Cloud-based identity management services are one of the highly demanded PaaS offerings from the cloud providers.

The next major security concern is data protection. In this chapter, we will cover some of the services available in Azure for data protection. Also, we will cover usage scenarios of the Azure Key Vault, which is a Key Management Store as a service.

Security Features of Azure SQL Database

Azure SQL Database has security in different layers. **It provides the firewall security for the logical database servers.** This is explained in Chapter 2. Apart from this network security, SQL Database has other in-built data protection mechanisms.

Transparent Data Encryption (TDE)

At the data protection level, Azure SQL Database has the Transparent Data Encryption (TDE). **TDE makes the data, backups, and the logs encrypted at rest.** The encryption keys are managed by Microsoft.

Navigate to the SQL Database (DashDocs database) in the Azure portal and click the 'Transparent data encryption'; this will open the TDE blade (Figure 6-1). We haven't enabled the TDE for this database, so select the 'ON' option and enable the TDE.

© Thurupathan Vijayakumar 2017

T. Vijayakumar, *Practical Azure Application Development*, DOI 10.1007/978-1-4842-2817-3_6

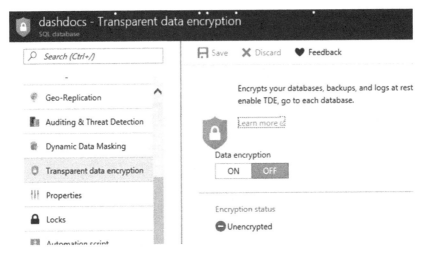

Figure 6-1. *SQL Database TDE blade*

This process will take some time depending the on the size of the database and geo replication.

As stated, TDE is fully managed by Microsoft. The encryption keys and key cycling are totally out of the scope of the owners. TDE is useful in order to adhere to the compliancy standards of the organizations. In TDE, data is encrypted at rest, not in transit, and the encryption is not visible to us.

Based on the TDE documentation (https://docs.microsoft.com/en-us/sql/ relational-databases/security/encryption/transparent-data-encryption-with- azure-sql-database) - **TDE encrypts the storage of the database using a symmetric key known as the database encryption key.** Database encryption keys are protected by a built-in server certificate; these certificates are unique for each SQL Database server. Microsoft cycles these certificates at least every 90 days.

■ **Note**   If you think of more fine-grained encryption for the database, we can implement the features like SQL Always Encrypted. You can read more about Always Encrypted feature from this link: https://docs.microsoft.com/en-us/sql/relational-databases/ security/encryption/always-encrypted-database-engine

Always Encrypted is a feature that encrypts the SQL Database data with custom keys with custom key management stores; the specialty is that data is encrypted both at rest and during transit.

You can read more about how to implement Always Encrypted in the Azure SQL Database using the Azure Key Vault as the key management store from this link: https://thuru. net/2016/03/03/provisioning-always-encrypted-in-sql-databases-with-azure- key-vault-using-ssms-2016/

Dynamic Data Masking

Dynamic Data Masking (DDM) is an SQL Server feature that masks the specified data during data retrieval. This is not an encryption option so the data at rest stays as it is.

Navigate to the SQL Database blade and click the 'Dynamic Data Masking' option. This will open the DDM blade (Figure 6-2). Note that sometimes Azure might suggest you mask the columns to apply DDM. In Figure 6-2 you can see Azure has suggested two columns FirstName and LastName to be masked.

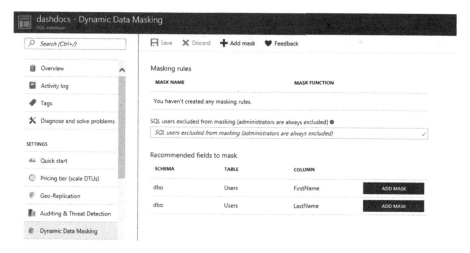

Figure 6-2. *Dynamic Data Masking blade*

You can also apply masking for the other columns (by clicking 'Add mask') and apply custom masking patterns as well.

■ **Note** Details of the DDM are not covered in this book since the portal does not provide the full experience of DDM.

You should use SSMS to test this feature with TSQL. You can read more about DDM from the following links.

```
https://msdn.microsoft.com/en-us/library/mt130841.aspx https://docs.
microsoft.com/en-us/azure/sql-database/sql-database-dynamic-data-masking-
get-started
```

Auditing and Threat Detection

SQL Database provides a detailed auditing and threat detection mechanism. This can either be enabled at the server level and all the databases inherit the settings from the server, or each database can have its own auditing and threat detection enabled as well.

In the SQL Database blade click the 'Auditing & Threat Detection' option (Figure 6-3). On the right-hand side, you can notice the check box 'Inherit settings from server' is checked, but the server auditing and threat detection is turned off.

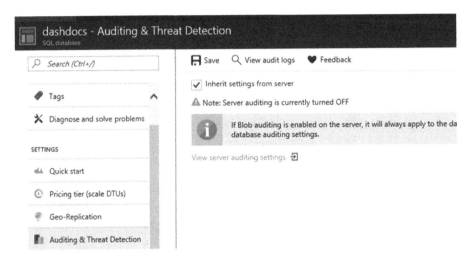

Figure 6-3. *SQL Database auditing and threat detection*

Uncheck the 'Inherit settings from server' and the blade will display the database auditing and threat detection options (Figure 6-4).

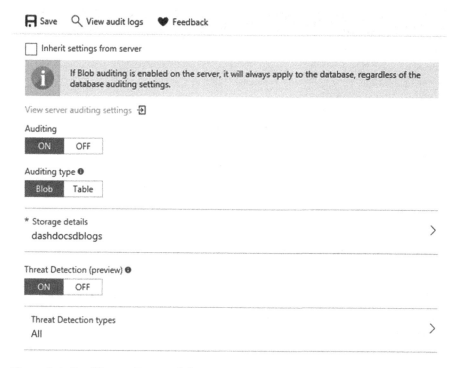

Figure 6-4. *Enabling auditing and threat detection for the database*

Set Auditing 'ON' and leave the Auditing type to Blob (choosing the auditing type to Table require you to change the connection strings of the clients including all the applications).

You should select an existing Blob storage or create a new one as the storage for the audit logs; you can also choose the number of days to retain the logs as well.

Set 'ON' for the Threat Detection (currently in preview); this will detect the potential threats and anomaly operations against the database and alert the administrators and specified users. Click the 'Threat Detection types' and you can select the threats you want to detect and to be notified. Finally, click 'Save' to save the settings.

Use the application or execute some commands against the database using SSMS, and open the 'Auditing and Threat Detection'; now you will see the logs (Figure 6-5). Click on a record and it will display the details of each TSQL command executed against the database.

Figure 6-5. SQL Database audit logs

■ **Note** SQL Databases have other additional security features like Row Level Security (RLS) and Always Encrypted. These options are heavily database dependent ones and not covered in this book.

Security Features of Azure Storage Services

Navigate to any storage accounts of the DashDocs application in the Azure portal (where we store the documents) and click the 'Encryption' option. This will open the storage account encryption blade (Figure 6-6).

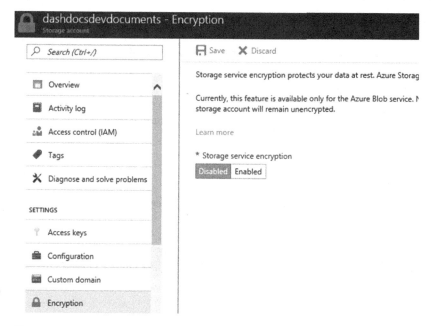

Figure 6-6. *Azure Storage encryption blade*

Like the TDE option of the SQL Databases, this is a very straightforward option; you have to specify whether to encrypt the storage or not. Currently the encryption is disabled.

Azure uses AES 256 encryption for the storage encryption. When the encryption option is enabled after the creation of the storage, the contents of the storage remain unencrypted until users access the data and save them back. This is applied when the encryption is disabled in the middle as well: contents will remain encrypted until users access the data and save them back.

We will not use the in-built storage encryption, as the next section covers the Azure Key Vault and how we can handle the encryption in the application itself.

Azure Key Vault

Azure Key Vault is a key management as a service, which not only has the ability to serve the software-based key management but also has the hardware-based key management via Hardware Security Modules (HSM).

137

We can either generate keys or import the existing keys to the Azure Key Vault. It has two options to manage the sensitive information.

1. Secrets – Key Vault accepts any value as a secret, and these are stored in binary. Sensitive pieces of information like passwords or API keys.

2. Keys – Keys are either generated by the Key Vault itself or imported. Keys are cryptographic and have public and private key pairs.

Provisioning Azure Key Vault

First, let's create an instance of Azure Key Vault. Search for Key Vault and select the option to create the Key Vault instance (Figure 6-7).

Figure 6-7. *Choosing Azure Key Vault to create*

This will open the Key Vault creation blade (Figure 6-8). Enter a name for your Key Vault, then select the resource group and the location of the Key Vault service. Select the pricing tier as 'Standard' as we will not use the HSM-based Key Vault.

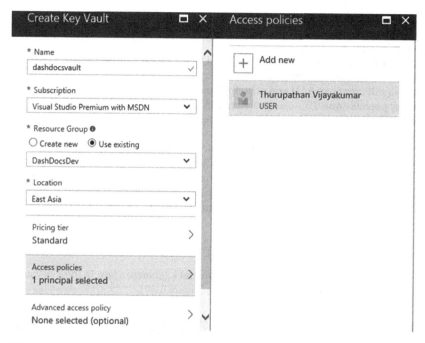

Figure 6-8. *Azure Key Vault creation blade*

Click Access Policies, and you can notice that the current user principal used to log in to the Azure portal has been selected. Click on the name of the user and it will open blade (Figure 6-9), which contains the Key Vault permissions for the selected principal.

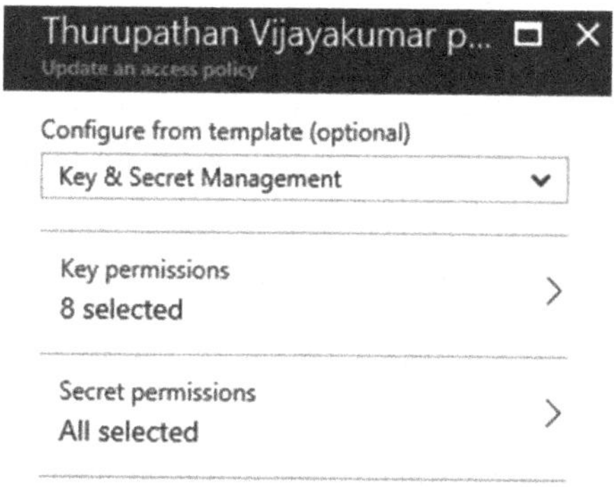

Figure 6-9. *Key Vault principal permissions*

There are some predefined templates for the principal permission management. Figure 6-9 shows that the current principal is configured with the 'Key & Secret Management' template.

It has eight key management permissions and all the secret management permissions. Let's leave the default options as it is.

Later we will create an AAD app principal and add that to the vault and grant required key permissions. This user principal will be used in the management operations of the Key Vault, and the AAD application principal will be used by the DashDocs application.

The last option of the Key Vault creation blade (Figure 6-8) is configuring the Advanced access policy. This is optional and has the options to specify whether the virtual machines and Azure Resource Manager have access to the Azure Key Vault. We will not require these additional access permissions for this practice, so leave the option as it is, click 'Create', and provision the new Key Vault instance.

Generating a Key in the Azure Key Vault

Navigate to the created Azure Key Vault instance and let's generate a key. In the Key Vault blade click 'Keys', and this will open the keys blade (Figure 6-10).

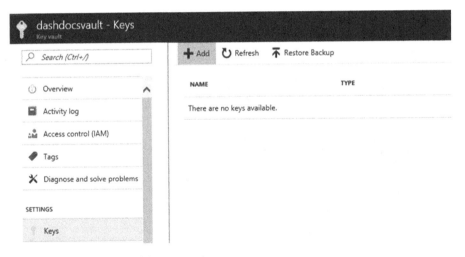

Figure 6-10. *Keys blade of the Key Vault*

Click the 'Add' option on top of the blade, and this will open the key creation blade (Figure 6-11).

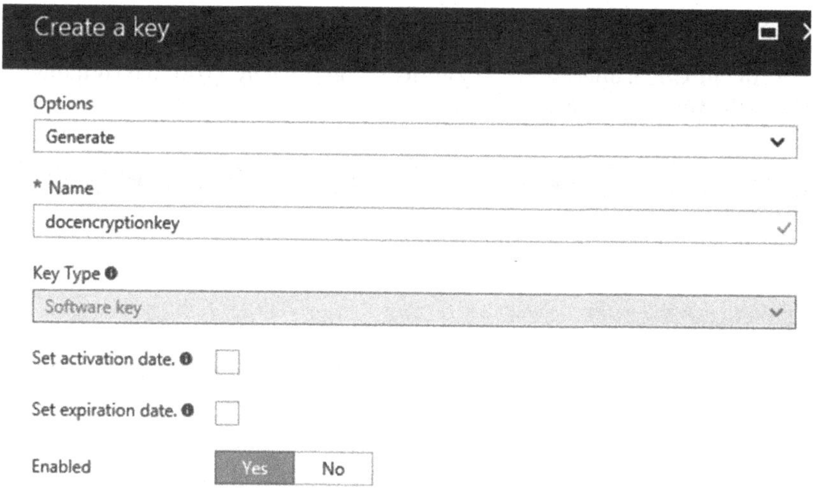

Figure 6-11. *Key creation blade*

There are three options to create a key in the Key Vault.

- Generate – Let the Key Vault generate a new key.

- Upload – Import an existing key to the Key Vault.

- Restore Backup – Restore a backup key generated by this Key Vault.

Select 'Generate' option and name the key. If required, we can set the activation and expiration of the key and additionally, we can enable and disable the key as well.

When you click 'Create', Azure Key Vault will provision a new key in the specified name. You can see the newly generated key in the keys blade (Figure 6-12).

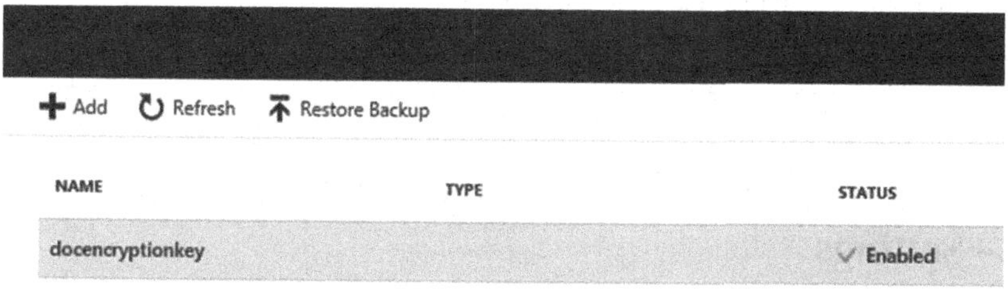

Figure 6-12. *List of keys in the keys blade*

141

Click the key and it will open the blade (Figure 6-13), which shows the versions of the key. Apparently, keys can have many versions and each version is generated under the same name. **An individual operational key entity is identified by a URI that contains the name and the version of the key**.

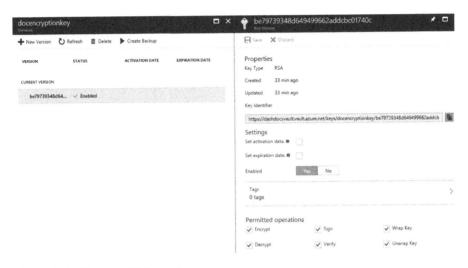

Figure 6-13. *Key record information*

Click on the version of the of the key and it will open the details of the key record as shown in Figure 6-13. Additionally, the blade shows the permitted operations of the key.

■ **Note**   Azure Key Vault trusts only Azure Active Directory authentications. The user principal, which is used to log into the Azure portal, has the permissions of the 'Key & Secret Management' template. If the logged-in user principal does not have those permissions, then the key generation and management operations cannot be performed through the portal by the logged-in user.

Azure Storage Client Side Encryption with Azure Key Vault – Settings

In order to enable the client side encryption, first we need an AAD principal to access the Azure Key Vault and perform cryptographic operations. Let's create an AAD principal. Navigate to the AAD blade and click the 'App registrations' (Figure 6-14).

Figure 6-14. *AAD app registrations blade*

Note, we have already registered an AAD application for the authentication purposes, so we can simply use this principal for this purpose, but it is not a good practice. So, we'll create a new dedicated AAD application for the Azure Key Vault access.

Click 'Add' to create a new application; this will open the AAD app creation blade (Figure 6-15).

Figure 6-15. *Create a new AAD app principal Key Vault access*

Create the AAD application, and navigate to the Azure Key Vault blade. Click the 'Access policies', and it will open the Key Vault access policies blade (Figure 6-16).

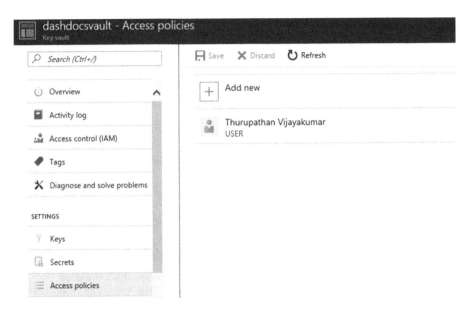

Figure 6-16. Key Vault access policies

You can notice that the user principal added during the creation of the Key Vault is in the list and now should add the AAD application principal to this list and configure the required permissions.

Click 'Add new' to add the AAD application. Then click the 'select principal', and it will open the blade to select the principal (Figure 6-17). Type the name of the app in the box and it will show up in the drop-down.

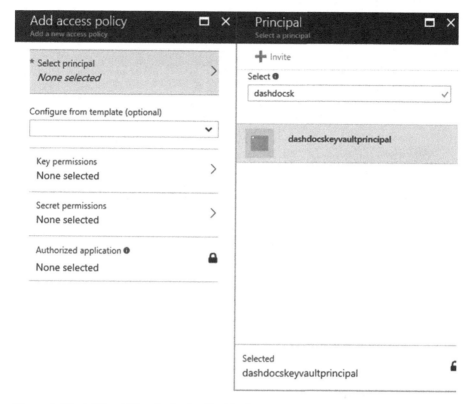

Figure 6-17. *Adding AAD principal to Key Vault*

Select the principal, and click the 'Key permissions'. It will open the key permissions blade (Figure 6-18), where we can assign the key permissions to this app. Since this app is going to be used in cryptographic operations, we will **select all the permissions under the cryptographic operations and the GET operation, which is required to retrieve the public parts of the key information.**

145

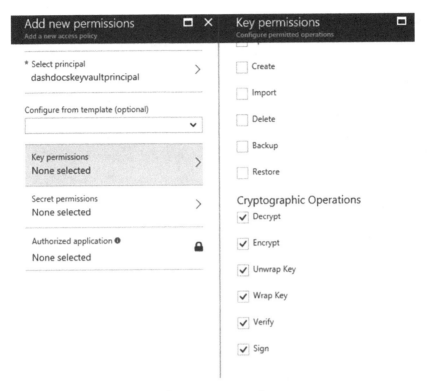

Figure 6-18. *Assign cryptographic permissions to the app*

Also, this principal does not require any permissions on secrets, so leave it blank. Finally click 'Ok' to add the new principal to the Key Vault access policies. In order to complete the action, you should click the 'Save' on top of the app policies blade.

In order to authenticate the application, we need to generate a secret key for the AAD application we created. **App secret will be used as the AAD authentication credential along with the application ID**.

Navigate to the AAD 'App registrations' section and select the app. This will open the app overview blade (Figure 6-19). Copy the application ID from this overview blade and keep it, as we will use the application ID in the code.

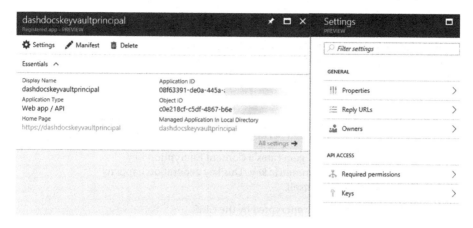

Figure 6-19. *AAD App overview blade*

Then click 'Keys' and this will open the app secret generation blade (Figure 6-20).

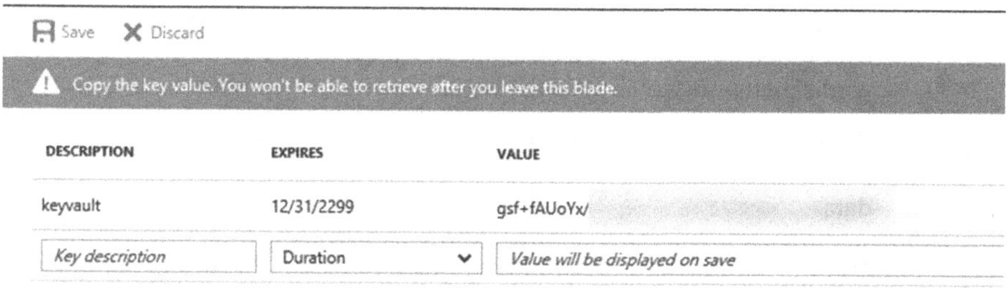

Figure 6-20. *AAD app secret generation blade*

Type a description for the secret and select the expiry period and click 'Save' on top of the blade. After the save, the secret value will show up in the blade; copy the value and keep it as we will use this in our code. **Note: this is the only time the key will be visible to you.**

Azure Storage Client Side Encryption with Azure Key Vault – Development

Let's begin the development and add the copied app secret and application ID in the app settings of the web.config.

```
<add key="KeyVault:AppId" value="<APPLICATION ID>"/>
<add key="KeyVault:AppSecret" value="<APPLICATION SECRET>"/>
```

Install the following packages.

```
Install-Package Microsoft.IdentityModel.Clients.ActiveDirectory
Install-Package Microsoft.Azure.KeyVault
Install-Package Microsoft.Azure.KeyVault.Extensions
```

Now, let's get into the details of how the Azure Storage client side encryption works with Azure Key Vault. **The client side encryption/decryption uses the envelope technique.** These are the steps that occur during the encryption/decryption process.

1. Azure Storage SDK generates a Content Encryption Key (CEK). This is a symmetric key. This key generation happens in the application itself.

2. The content will be encrypted by the CEK.

3. CEK will be encrypted by the Azure Key Vault key – Azure Key Vault key is the Key Encryption Key (KEK). The storage SDK does not have access to the KEK; it sends the CEK to the Azure Key Vault and gets it encrypted by the KEK. Storage SDK uses the AAD application authentication and retrieved access token to communicate and invoke the Azure Key Vault operations. So from the Azure Key Vault's point of view, the application principal is the party who invokes the operations.

4. The encrypted content along with the encrypted CEK, KEK path, and additional metadata will be stored in the blob meta data.

5. When retrieving the information, the encrypted content along with the metadata will be downloaded to the client.

6. Azure Storage SDK reads the metadata, authenticates it to the Azure Key Vault, and gets the CEK decrypted by sending the encrypted CEK content stored in the metadata.

7. Then it uses the decrypted CEK to decrypt the content.

Each storage service (Table, Blobs, Queues) uses different encryption strategies for the content encryption by the CEK. You can read more about it from this link: `https://docs.microsoft.com/en-us/azure/storage/storage-client-side-encryption`.

Now that we're all set for the client encryption, we need to modify the BlobStorageService.cs class. Copy the Key identifier URI from the key record information blade (Figure 6-13) and place it as private constant string in the BlobStorageService class.

```
private const string KEY_URI = "https://dashdocsvault.vault.azure.net/keys/
docencryptionkey/be79739348d649499662addcbc01740c";
```

Add a private method that handles the authentication of the AAD application and retrieve the access_token. This access_token will be used by the storage SDK to invoke the Azure Key Vault operations.

```
private async static Task<string> GetToken(string authority, string
resource, string scope)
        {
            var appId = ConfigurationManager.AppSettings["KeyVault:AppId"].
            ToString();
            var appSecret = ConfigurationManager.AppSettings["KeyVault:AppSe
            cret"].ToString();

            var authContext = new AuthenticationContext(authority);
            var clientCredentials = new ClientCredential(appId, appSecret);

            var result = authContext.AcquireTokenAsync(resource,
            clientCredentials).GetAwaiter().GetResult();
            return result.AccessToken;
        }
```

Then modify the UploadDocumentAsync method with the following code.

```
public async Task<string> UploadDocumentAsync(HttpPostedFileBase
documentFile, Guid customerId, Guid documentId)
        {
            var storageAccount = CloudStorageAccount.
            Parse(ConfigurationManager.ConnectionStrings["DocumentStore"].
            ConnectionString);
            var blobClient = storageAccount.CreateCloudBlobClient();

            var container = blobClient.GetContainerReference(customerId.
            ToString().ToLower());
            await container.CreateIfNotExistsAsync();

            var keyvaultResolver = new KeyVaultKeyResolver(GetToken);
            var key = await keyvaultResolver.ResolveKeyAsync
            (KEY_URI, CancellationToken.None);

            var encryptionPolicy = new BlobEncryptionPolicy(key, null);
            var requestOptions = new BlobRequestOptions
            { EncryptionPolicy = encryptionPolicy };

            var blobRelativePath = documentId.ToString().ToLower() + "/" +
            Path.GetFileName(documentFile.FileName).ToLower();

            var block = container.GetBlockBlobReference(blobRelativePath);

            await block.UploadFromStreamAsync(documentFile.InputStream,
            documentFile.InputStream.Length, null, requestOptions, null);

            return blobRelativePath;
        }
```

We construct the BlobRequestOptions object and pass that to the UploadFromStreamAsync method. This option parameter contains the information to enforce the encryption before upload.

Let's modify the DownloadDocumentAsync to decrypt the content.

```
public async Task<KeyValuePair<string, MemoryStream>>
DownloadDocumentAsync(Guid documentId, Guid customerId)
        {
            var storageAccount = CloudStorageAccount.
            Parse(ConfigurationManager.ConnectionStrings["DocumentStore"].
            ConnectionString);
            var blobClient = storageAccount.CreateCloudBlobClient();

            var container = blobClient.GetContainerReference(customerId.
            ToString().ToLower());

            var dbContext = new DashDocsContext();
            var document = await dbContext.Documents.SingleAsync
            (d => d.Id == documentId);

            var keyvaultResolver = new KeyVaultKeyResolver(GetToken);

            var encryptionPolicy = new BlobEncryptionPolicy
            (null, keyvaultResolver);
            var requestOptions = new BlobRequestOptions
            { EncryptionPolicy = encryptionPolicy };

            var block = container.GetBlockBlobReference(document.BlobPath);

            var stream = new MemoryStream();
            await block.DownloadToStreamAsync(stream, null,
            requestOptions, null);

            var content = new KeyValuePair<string, MemoryStream>
            (document.DocumentName, stream);

            return content;
        }
```

Note, in the DownloadDocumentAsync method we did not use the KEY_URI property, because the encrypted content itself has this property in its metadata and storage so SDK will reference to that.

The complete BlobStorageService.cs

```
public class BlobStorageService
    {
        private const string KEY_URI = "https://dashdocsvault.vault.azure.
        net/keys/docencryptionkey/be79739348d649499662addcbc01740c";
```

```
public async Task<string> UploadDocumentAsync(HttpPostedFileBase
documentFile, Guid customerId, Guid documentId)
{
    var storageAccount = CloudStorageAccount.
    Parse(ConfigurationManager.ConnectionStrings["DocumentStore"].
    ConnectionString);
    var blobClient = storageAccount.CreateCloudBlobClient();

    var container = blobClient.GetContainerReference(customerId.
    ToString().ToLower());
    await container.CreateIfNotExistsAsync();

    var keyvaultResolver = new KeyVaultKeyResolver(GetToken);
    var key = await keyvaultResolver.ResolveKeyAsync(KEY_URI,
    CancellationToken.None);

    var encryptionPolicy = new BlobEncryptionPolicy(key, null);
    var requestOptions = new BlobRequestOptions
    { EncryptionPolicy = encryptionPolicy };

    var blobRelativePath = documentId.ToString().ToLower() + "/" +
    Path.GetFileName(documentFile.FileName).ToLower();

    var block = container.GetBlockBlobReference(blobRelativePath);

    await block.UploadFromStreamAsync(documentFile.InputStream,
    documentFile.InputStream.Length, null, requestOptions, null);

    return blobRelativePath;
}

public async Task<KeyValuePair<string, MemoryStream>>
DownloadDocumentAsync(Guid documentId, Guid customerId)
{
    var storageAccount = CloudStorageAccount.
    Parse(ConfigurationManager.ConnectionStrings["DocumentStore"].
    ConnectionString);
    var blobClient = storageAccount.CreateCloudBlobClient();

    var container = blobClient.GetContainerReference
    (customerId.ToString().ToLower());

    var dbContext = new DashDocsContext();
    var document = await dbContext.Documents.SingleAsync
    (d => d.Id == documentId);

    var keyvaultResolver = new KeyVaultKeyResolver(GetToken);
```

151

```
            var encryptionPolicy = new BlobEncryptionPolicy(null,
            keyvaultResolver);
            var requestOptions = new BlobRequestOptions
            { EncryptionPolicy = encryptionPolicy };

            var block = container.GetBlockBlobReference(document.BlobPath);

            var stream = new MemoryStream();
            await block.DownloadToStreamAsync(stream, null, requestOptions,
            null);

            var content = new KeyValuePair<string, MemoryStream>(document.
            DocumentName, stream);

            return content;
        }

        private async static Task<string> GetToken(string authority, string
        resource, string scope)
        {
            var appId = ConfigurationManager.AppSettings["KeyVault:AppId"].
            ToString();
            var appSecret = ConfigurationManager.AppSettings["KeyVault:AppSe
            cret"].ToString();

            var authContext = new AuthenticationContext(authority);
            var clientCredentials = new ClientCredential(appId, appSecret);

            var result = authContext.AcquireTokenAsync(resource,
            clientCredentials).GetAwaiter().GetResult();
            return result.AccessToken;
        }
    }
```

Run the application, and upload a document, then download it. You will see no difference as the document is uploaded and downloaded as earlier, but now the contents of Blob are encrypted from the web application before they hit the Azure Blob storage and also the contents of the Blob are read in the encrypted format and decrypted in the web application before the download.

In order to check the encryption, open the Windows Storage Explorer (a desktop to tool to manage Azure Storage) introduced in Chapter 2 (you can download it here: http://storageexplorer.com/). Add the respective Blob storage and navigate to the container and right-click on the newly uploaded file and select 'Properties' (Figure 6-21).

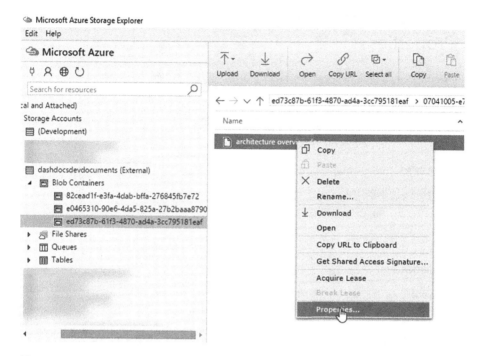

Figure 6-21. Viewing properties of the blob using Azure Storage Explorer

This will open the properties dialog of the Blob. You can find encryption data under the Metadata section (Figure 6-22).

Figure 6-22. *Blob encryption metadata*

View the encryption metadata - you will get something similar to the below information.

```
{"EncryptionMode":"FullBlob","WrappedContentKey":{"KeyId":"https://
dashdocsvault.vault.azure.net/keys/docencryptionkey/be79739348d649499662add
cbc01740c","EncryptedKey":"EGW+RuZYkJuhzekx75kic1miGyIoZist3pTkMLld1sGbANw
TUoZqwrTJG8rE5+Gz7oe8I7lZIYODlU4Pd8I2FuhA9/wwOduMRy2+QqZoiHQK3v7oXI1vL4ReOm
xvfdbyISpvcBxijrLc39Z3Co7wLWKy1lGGXZQf8AN6hLUMLwxLr9vj6oE/cweRMH6nBPEfoCj4p
x5OPecYOlZtltOUjZHjeeoUfVyiPTyGxR1uKMhq1nX1c+PL32BOx7GYd7njFFgENQV4rEQQDuId
wd41+SmLLr2XcXZCfaAxOOjfEATPaoBkEbOMOFJKM2jLKO8anf/RoBeg/VyVKLS4usAMow==",
"Algorithm":"RSA-OAEP"},"EncryptionAgent":{"Protocol":"1.0","Encryption
Algorithm":"AES_CBC_256"},"ContentEncryptionIV":"iY4ji81fFZdXlaZtBMn2lQ==","
KeyWrappingMetadata":{"EncryptionLibrary":".NET 8.0.0"}}
```

You can notice that the metadata includes the information of the Azure Key Vault key identifier, encryption mode, encrypted key (CEK), etc.

■ **Note** In the above practice, in order to keep the brevity, we have used one key for all the customers of the application. In real scenarios, we will have different keys and different key expirations and key generation policies for each customer. And the key identifiers will be persisted in the application database.

Summary

This chapter provided sufficient information about the general security guidelines and features of Azure and a detailed overview of the Azure Key Vault and Azure Storage client side encryption. Get the source code for this chapter from `https://github.com/thuru/DashDocs/tree/master/DashDocs/Chapter%206`.

The choice of the services and to which level we require security is always a tradeoff between the cost and the essentiality of the security for the specific business domain. You have to consider the nature of the business, the usage, and information sensitivity when deciding the security options.

Figure 6-23 shows the current state of the application.

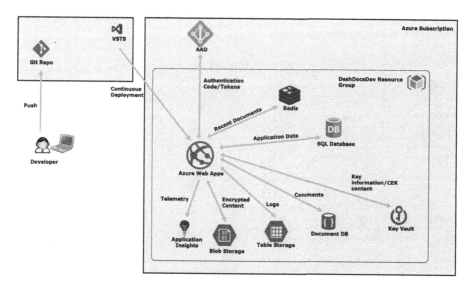

Figure 6-23. *DashDocs application overview*

CHAPTER 7

■ ■ ■

Integrating Azure Search

Search is an essential part of any application; sometimes search defines the entire functionality of an application as well. Azure Search is a search-as-a service model, where the management of search resources is handled by Azure and developers are left to focus on the search functionality.

Azure Search has rich capabilities like multi-lingual search support, document cracking, in-built indexing support for various data sources, search suggestions, hit-highlighting, faceted navigation, geo-spatial search, and much more. The broader spectrum of features provided in an Azure search makes it a perfect choice for various workloads in web and mobile application development. Azure Search supports Apache Lucene query syntax as well.

In this chapter, we'll integrate the Azure Search to the application and enable the search functionality. Like other Azure services, Azure Search is also a very comprehensive service with many features and settings. This chapter covers the core aspects of the Azure Search, sufficient enough to begin the search journey with Azure Search.

Azure Search Components

Azure Search has many components and various configurations for each feature. The following list shows the fundamental components of Azure Search, which are mandatory to get started.

- Search Service SKU – Like other Azure services, Azure Search also comes in different pricing and capacity models. Choosing the SKU is a careful decision because you cannot change the SKU later. In case of upgrade you have to re-create your indexes, search rules, etc.

- Search Index – This is the search database; search queries are executed against the search index and results are retrieved. Search index has documents. Each document is an individually searchable item in the search index.

- Search Indexer – The scheduler that connects to the data sources and updates the search index.

© Thurupathan Vijayakumar 2017
T. Vijayakumar, *Practical Azure Application Development*, DOI 10.1007/978-1-4842-2817-3_7

- • Data source – Data source is the real or the origin of the searchable data. Azure Search supports different data sources like SQL Database, Document DB, SQL Database on VMs, Azure Blob Storage, and Azure Table Storage.

Provisioning an Azure Search Service

Navigate to the Azure portal and search for the Azure Search service (Figure 7-1). Choose Azure Search to provision the search instance.

Figure 7-1. *Choosing Azure Search service*

This will open the Azure Search service creation blade (Figure 7-2).

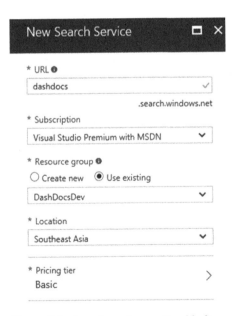

Figure 7-2. *Search service creation blade*

Fill in the required information and select a pricing tier (Search service SKU). Each tier has capacity in terms of number of indexes, total number of documents, and storage. Higher tiers have the options of having replicas and partitions for the scalability. You can read more about the Search service SKU tiers from this link: `https://docs.microsoft.com/en-us/azure/search/search-sku-tier`

Also, note that **changing the service SKU tier of the Azure Search will result in creating the indexes and populating them from the beginning**. There's no such technique as index migration.

After filling in all the required information, click to provision the search service.

Creating a Search Index and Import Data

Before getting started with search indexes and data import, first we should define the search functionality from the application perspective. In order to keep the brevity, let's plan the search in terms of document name and owner. **Also, we should apply the customer filter in search results.**

Azure Search supports SQL Database as a data source and it expects the required data to be listed in a single table or view. In order to support the search indexing we will create a view in the database.

Create a new view named 'AllDocuments' in the database. You can execute the below TSQL statement in order to create the view.

```
CREATE VIEW [dbo].[AllDocuments] AS
SELECT
D.Id AS 'DocumentId', D.DocumentName, U.FirstName, U.LastName, C.Id AS
'CustomerId', D.CreatedOn
FROM Documents AS D
JOIN Users AS U ON U.Id = D.OwnerId
JOIN Customers AS C ON U.CustomerId = C.Id
```

Now, navigate to the Azure Search service and click the 'Import Data' button (Figure 7-3).

Figure 7-3. *Search service overview blade with Import Data button on top*

This will open the Import Data blade (Figure 7-4).

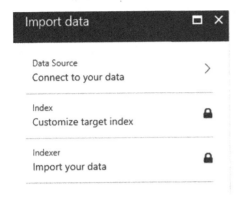

Figure 7-4. *Import Data blade*

Select Data source option from the blade, and this will open the blade with the different data sources supported by the Azure Search index (Figure 7-5).

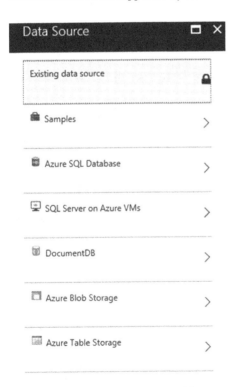

Figure 7-5. *Data sources supported by Azure Search*

Choose Azure SQL Database, and it will open the blade (Figure 7-6) to configure the data source connection.

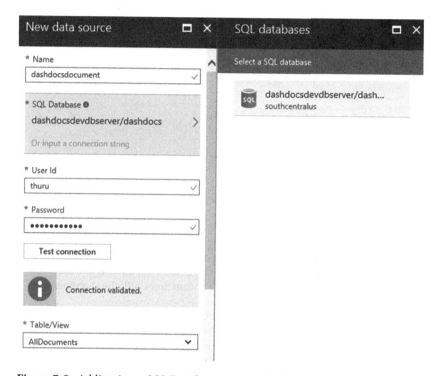

Figure 7-6. *Adding Azure SQL Database as a search data source*

Enter a name for the data source – **the name should be in lowercase.** And select the 'SQL Database' section; another blade will appear with the available list of SQL Databases. Optionally you can specify a connection string as well.

Enter the username and password to access the SQL Database. You can test the connection, and once the connection has been validated the blade will show the list of tables and views from the database. Select the 'AllDocuments' view from the drop-down and click 'Ok' to complete.

This will add the data source and since we're doing this via the portal, the portal will sample the data and open the Index section with an autogenerated index populate with the names of fields from the view (Figure 7-7).

* Index name ❶

documentindex

* Key ❶

DocumentId

Basic   Analyzer   Suggester

FIELD NAME	TYPE	RETRIEVABLE ☐	FILTERABLE ☐	SORTABLE ☐	FACETABLE ☐	SEARCHABLE ☐
DocumentId	Edm.String	☑	☐	☐	☐	☐
DocumentName	Edm.String	☑	☐	☐	☐	☑
FirstName	Edm.String	☑	☐	☐	☐	☑
LastName	Edm.String	☑	☐	☐	☐	☐
CustomerId	Edm.String	☑	☑	☐	☐	☐
CreatedOn	Edm.DateTimeOffset	☑	☐	☑	☐	

Figure 7-7. *Creating search index*

Name your index (this should be lowercase), and select the Key – In this scenario
the key for each search document is the Document Id. **Search documents are the
individual entities of the search index,** so do not confuse them with the Documents of
the application.

In the field matrix, mark the fields RETRIEVABLE that you want to be included in the
search results – we have marked all the fields as retrievable. Mark the DocumentName
and FirstName as SEARCHABLE – this ensures these two fields in the search documents
are searchable with the specific analyzer.

Mark CustomerId as FILTERABLE – we will apply the filter on this field in order
to restrict the search results to the specific customer. CreatedOn field is marked as
SORTABLE as this is a good sort candidate.

Click the 'Analyzer' tab (Figure 7-8), and note the searchable fields are marked with
the Standard-Lucene analyzer. We can use Apache Lucene query syntax to search against
these fields. Read more about Apache Lucene syntax from this link: `https://lucene.`
`apache.org/core/2_9_4/queryparsersyntax.html`.

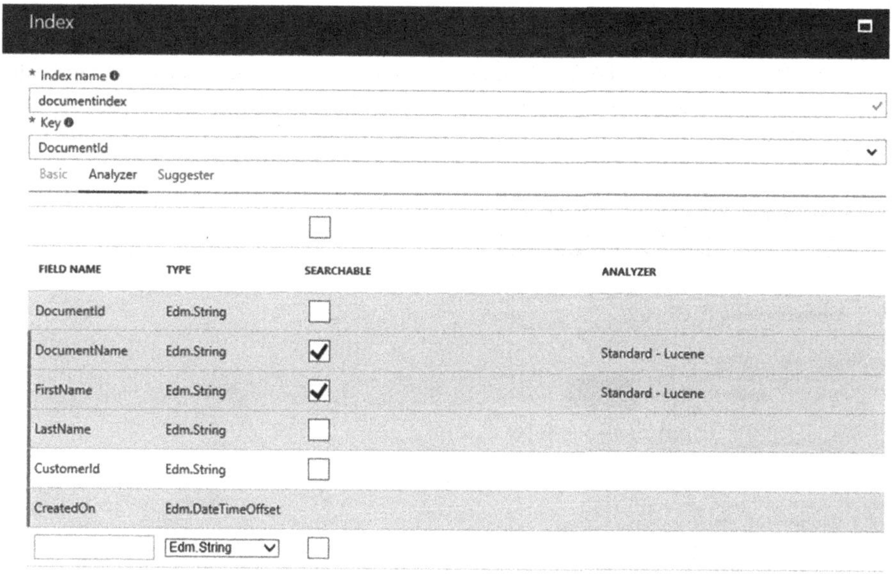

Figure 7-8. *Search Index analyzer*

Click the 'Suggester' tab (Figure 7-9) and you can configure the search suggestions. Suggestions are simple as when the user types a part of the search term, then Azure Search will list the suggestions.

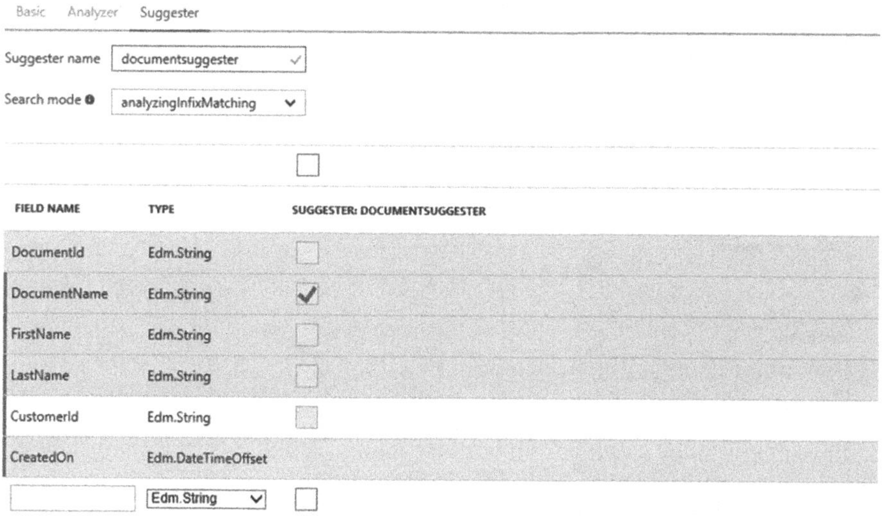

Figure 7-9. *Search Index suggester*

Name the suggester and select DocumentName field to enable suggestions. This will trigger the Azure Search to provide a list of suggestions from the DocumentName field.

Click 'Ok' to complete the search index creation process. Next, the Indexer blade will open (Figure 7-10). Indexer is the scheduler that scans the data sources and updates the search index.

Figure 7-10. *Search Indexer blade*

Enter a name for the Indexer, and under Schedule you can configure the schedule frequency, choose the custom schedule, and give a time period for the scheduler in the Interval section (5 minutes is the minimum). This is the frequency the Indexer runs and updates the search index.

Enter the Start time in the UTC standard for the Indexer to begin the first execution. **The high watermark column field represents the column that indicates the last updated data of the row, timestamp, or version number (the values get incremented on each updated); columns are best suited here.**

Here we have selected CreatedOn column; this is fairly a static choice – The reason for this because we do not have a column to track the updates in this sample.

If you check the 'Track deletions' check box, you will be asked to select the 'Soft delete column' and the 'Delete marker value'. These are straightforward as we have to select the soft delete column and the value that marks the row as deleted. Example, a column name IsDeleted would be a soft delete column where if it has the value 'true' deletion has happened.

We will not use this option, since we do not have a soft delete column in our application.

Click on the 'Advanced options' and it will open the advanced options configuring blade (Figure 7-11).

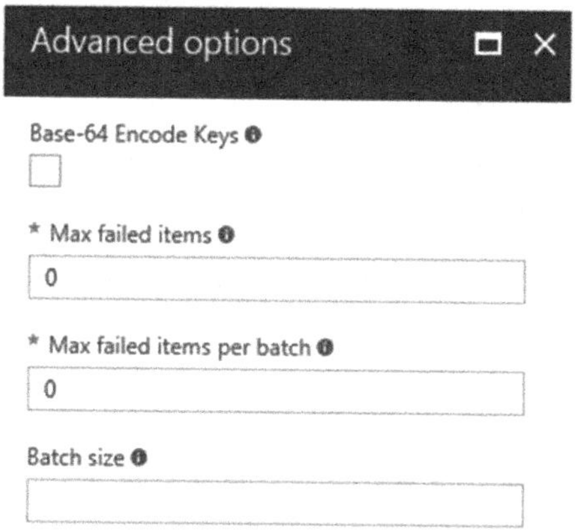

Figure 7-11. *Search Indexer advanced options*

We can configure the advanced options in this blade; check the 'Base-64 Encode Keys' if the index key has special characters like slashes and spaces. We can configure the maximum number of failed items to consider any Indexer run as a failure, also we can add thresholds for the maximum number of failed items per batch and the batch size in order to consider an Indexer run as a failure.

Click 'Ok' and finalize the Search Index and Indexer creation. By completing the above set of activities, we have created an Azure Search Index and an associated Indexer. After the completion, Azure Search will sample the data, and a few minutes later you can see the index has been populated with the number of documents in the database (Figure 7-12).

Indexes		
NAME	DOCUMENT COUNT	STORAGE SIZE
documentindex	41	59.66 KiB

Figure 7-12. *Azure Index with populated search documents*

■ **Note** We have used the portal to configure search options like constructing the Indexer, loading data, and setting up the Indexer. Using the Azure Search SDK, we can perform these actions in a more granular and specific way.

Testing Azure Search via Portal

Azure portal not only offers the search configuration experience, but it also offers a simple straightforward experience to test the search. Now we have the search index ready and populated, so we can try the search via portal.

Navigate to the Azure search blade, and click on the index (Figure 7-12). This will open the search index blade (Figure 7-13).

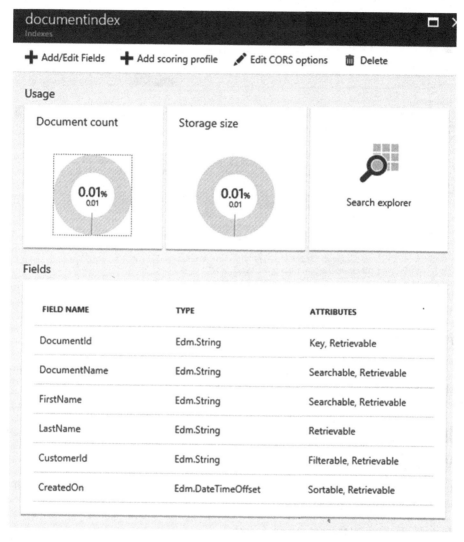

Figure 7-13. *Search index blade*

Click the 'Search explorer' in the search index blade, and this will open the search explorer blade (Figure 7-14). You can type search terms and options in this blade and test the search in the portal.

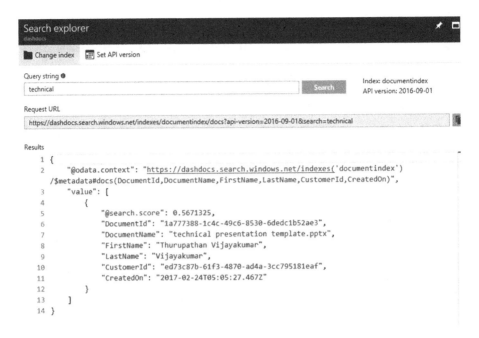

Figure 7-14. *Search explorer blade*

We can try different search terms and conditions with the Lucene search syntax and check the search.

Integrating Azure Search to the Application via SDK

In this section let's focus on integrating Azure Search to the DashDocs application. Install the following NuGet package.

```
Install-Package Microsoft.Azure.Search
```

We need to retrieve the Search service query key from the portal. Navigate to the Search blade and click on the 'Keys'; this will open the Search keys blade (Figure 7-15).

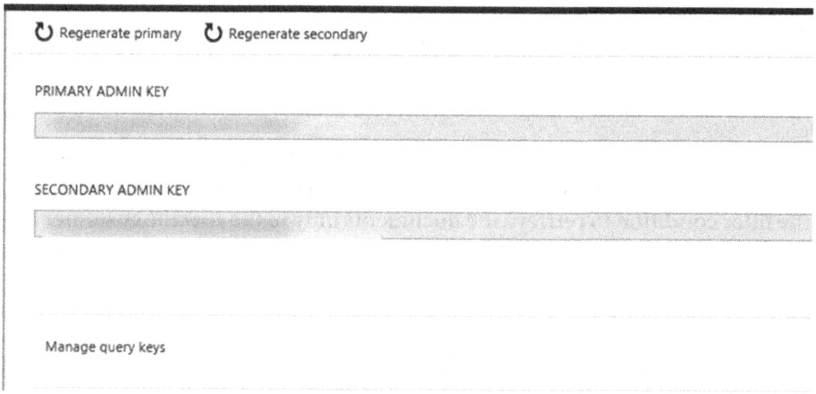

Figure 7-15. *Search keys blade*

You will see the Azure Search management keys, which you can use for setting up the search indexes, loading search data, setting up the indexers, etc. But in this case, we require the search query keys, which have only the query permissions.

Click on the 'Manage query keys' and it will open a new blade that has the query keys (Figure 7-16).

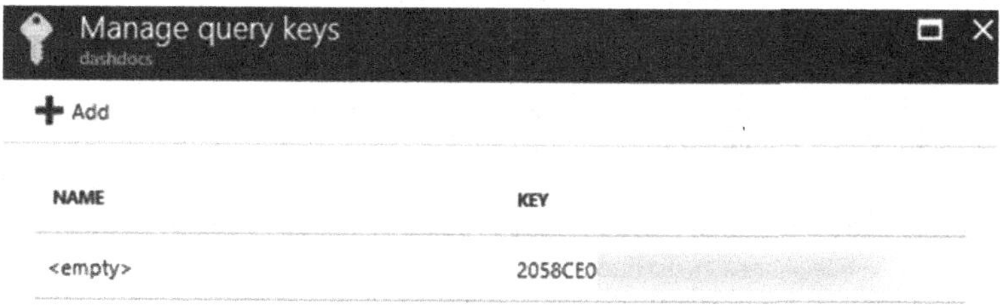

Figure 7-16. *Search query keys blade*

You can create a new key or use the default with the empty name. Copy this key and let's store this in the web.config app settings.

```
<add key="Search:ServiveKey" value="<SEARCH QUERY KEY>"/>
```

Now we need to create a model class that represents the search index. Create a class called DocumentIndex under the Models folder.

DocumentIndex.cs

```
public class DocumentIndex
    {
        public Guid DocumentId { get; set; }
        public Guid CustomerId { get; set; }
        public string DocumentName { get; set; }
```

```
        public string FirstName { get; set; }
        public string LastName { get; set; }
        public DateTime CreatedOn { get; set; }
    }
```

Create a class named SearchService under the Services folder and a simple method to perform searches against the search index we created. **In the application, we will impose the filter condition to retrieve the documents only to the specific customer Id.**

SearchService.cs

```
public class SearchService
    {
        private static ISearchIndexClient _searchIndexClient;

        static SearchService()
        {
            var searchServiceName = "dashdocs";
            var indexName = "documentindex";
            var searchApiKey = ConfigurationManager.AppSettings["Search:Serv
            iveKey"].ToString();

            _searchIndexClient = new SearchIndexClient(searchServiceName,
            indexName, new SearchCredentials(searchApiKey));
        }

        public async Task<List<DocumentIndex>> SearchAsync(string
        searchTerm, Guid customerId)
        {
            var parameters = new SearchParameters
            {
                Filter = $"CustomerId eq '{customerId.ToString().
                ToLower()}'",
                OrderBy = new[] { "CreatedOn desc"}
            };

            var searchResult = await _searchIndexClient.Documents.SearchAsyn
            c<DocumentIndex>(searchTerm.ToLower(), parameters);

            return new List<DocumentIndex>(searchResult.Results.Select(s =>
            s.Document));
        }
    }
```

Create a controller named SearchController with a single action method, which has the function to connect to the SearchService and get the results.

SearchController.cs

```
[Authorize]
    public class SearchController : DashDocsControllerBase
    {
        public async Task<ActionResult> Index(string search)
        {
            var documents = new List<DocumentIndex>();

            if(Request.QueryString["search"] != null)
            {
                var searchService = new SearchService();
                documents = await searchService.SearchAsync(search,
                DashDocsClaims.CustomerId);
            }

            return View(documents);
        }
    }
```

This action method receives the search term in the query string and passes that to the SearchAsync method of the SearchService class along with the customer Id. This customer Id is used as the filter parameter in the search.

Now, let's add a corresponding view to be used in the search and display the results. This view will have the grid of the documents similar to the Home/Index view with the action links Details & Download.

Search/Index.cshtml

```
@model IEnumerable<DashDocs.Models.DocumentIndex>

<div class="col-md-12 bg-blue">
    @{
        ViewBag.Title = "Documents Search";
    }
</div>

<div class="col-md-12 page-content">
    <div class="col-md-12 no-padding">
        @using (Html.BeginForm("Index", "Search", FormMethod.Get))
        {
            <div class="form-group padding-top-25">
                <label class="control-label ">Search : </label>
                <div class="col-md-12 no-padding">
                    <input type="text" name="search" id="search" />
                </div>
            </div>
```

```html
        <div class="form-group">
            <div class="col-md-10 padding-tb-15">
                <input type="submit" value="Search" class="btn btn-
                primary" />
            </div>
        </div>
    }
</div>

<div class="col-md-12 div-table">
    <h2>Results</h2>
    <table class="table table-hover">
        <tr>
            <th>
                Document Name
            </th>
            <th>
                Owner
            </th>
            <th>
                Created On
            </th>
            <th></th>
        </tr>
        <tbody>
            @foreach (var item in Model)
            {
                <tr>
                    <td>
                        @Html.DisplayFor(modelItem => item.DocumentName)
                    </td>
                    <td>
                        @Html.DisplayFor(modelItem => item.FirstName)
                    </td>
                    <td>
                        @Html.DisplayFor(modelItem => item.CreatedOn)
                    </td>
                    <td>
                        @Html.ActionLink("Details", "Index", "Document",
                        new { documentId = item.DocumentId }, new { }) |
                        @Html.ActionLink("Download", "Download", "Home",
                        new { documentId = item.DocumentId })
```

```
                </td>
            </tr>
        }
        </tbody>
    </table>

    </div>

</div>
```

The view has a text input to enter the search term and the results are shown in the grid. Figure 7-17 shows the application search view.

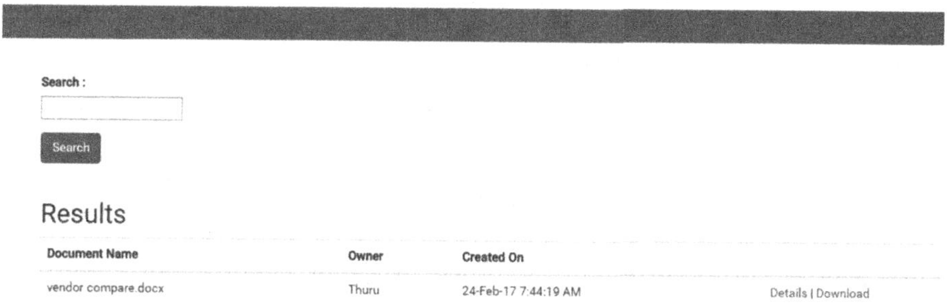

Figure 7-17. *Search view of the application*

Summary

We have completed the Azure Search service integration in the DashDocs application. We provisioned the service and configured it using the Azure portal.

Figure 7-18 shows the current overview of the DashDocs application and you can download the source code for this chapter from this https://github.com/thuru/DashDocs/tree/master/DashDocs/Chapter%207.

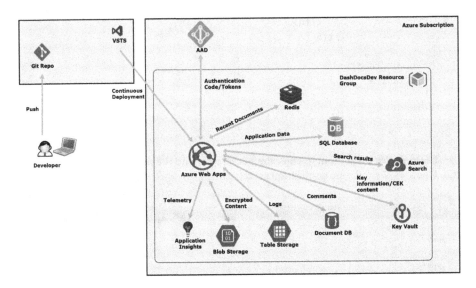

Figure 7-18. *DashDocs application overview*

In the next chapter, we will create Power BI reports for the document download data and embed those interactive reports inside the DashDocs application using the Azure Power BI Embedded service.

▓ ▓ ▓

CHAPTER 8

Data Visualization with Power BI Embedded

Power BI Embedded is the famous Power BI as a service in Azure. It allows us to have rich interactive data visualizations embedded in custom applications, without the requirement of having separate Power BI related licenses. The entire service is managed by Azure, and we can use the familiar Power BI desktop tools to create the reports.

This chapter covers the three major steps of using Power BI Embedded in your applications – creating reports, exporting them to Azure Power BI Embedded workspace, and embedding them in your applications.

Creating Power BI Reports Using Power BI Desktop

Let's create a Power BI report to show the download data of the documents. In order to create this Power BI report, first we need to prepare the data – we should make modifications in the current DashDocs application, to collect the download information.

Set the Application Models for Reporting Purposes

We will have a log table that holds the download information of each document. We will record the Document ID and the date of the download as vital information along with Customer ID. Each download will add a record to this table.

Let's add a new model class DocumentDownload, and add it to the DashDocsContext and trigger EF migration and update the database.

DocumentDownload.cs

```
public class DocumentDownload
    {
        [Key]
        public Guid Id { get; set; }
```

© Thurupathan Vijayakumar 2017
T. Vijayakumar, *Practical Azure Application Development*, DOI 10.1007/978-1-4842-2817-3_8

```
        [ForeignKey("Document")]
        public Guid DocumentId { get; set; }

        public DateTime DownloadedOn { get; set; }

        public Guid CustomerId { get; set; }

        [ForeignKey("DocumentId")]
        public virtual Document Document { get; set; }
    }
```

DashDocsContext.cs

```
public class DashDocsContext : DbContext
    {
        public DashDocsContext()
        {
        }

        public DbSet<Customer> Customers { get; set; }
        public DbSet<User> Users { get; set; }
        public DbSet<Document> Documents { get; set; }
        public DbSet<DocumentDownload> DocumentDownloads { get; set; }
    }
```

We should alter the DownloadDocumentAsync method in the BlobStorageService class to insert the DocumentDownload record.

```
public async Task<KeyValuePair<string, MemoryStream>>
DownloadDocumentAsync(Guid documentId, Guid customerId)
        {
            var storageAccount = CloudStorageAccount.
            Parse(ConfigurationManager.ConnectionStrings["DocumentStore"].
            ConnectionString);
            var blobClient = storageAccount.CreateCloudBlobClient();

            var container = blobClient.GetContainerReference(customerId.
            ToString().ToLower());

            var dbContext = new DashDocsContext();
            var document = await dbContext.Documents.SingleAsync(d =>
            d.Id == documentId);

            var keyvaultResolver = new KeyVaultKeyResolver(GetToken);

            var encryptionPolicy = new BlobEncryptionPolicy(null,
            keyvaultResolver);
```

```
var requestOptions = new BlobRequestOptions { EncryptionPolicy =
encryptionPolicy };

var block = container.GetBlockBlobReference(document.BlobPath);

var stream = new MemoryStream();
await block.DownloadToStreamAsync(stream, null, requestOptions,
null);

var content = new KeyValuePair<string, MemoryStream>(document.
DocumentName, stream);

// non blocking download data insert
dbContext.DocumentDownloads.Add(
    new DocumentDownload
    {
        Id = Guid.NewGuid(),
        DocumentId = document.Id,
        CustomerId = customerId,
        DownloadedOn = DateTime.UtcNow.Date,

    });
dbContext.SaveChangesAsync();

return content;
}
```

Add the database migration and update the database using the following commands in the Package Manager Console.

```
Add-Migration AddDocumentDownloadTable
Update-Database
```

Once completed, run the application and download some documents, and this will populate the DocumentDownloads table, which we can use alongside the data from the Documents table to create the report.

Creating the Power BI Report

In order to create the reports, we should install Power BI desktop. Go to https:// powerbi.microsoft.com/en-us/desktop/ and download the Power BI Desktop tool and install it in your PC.

Launch the Power BI Desktop application and click the 'Get Data' option in the ribbon and choose SQL Server; this will open a window to enter the SQL Server name and the database (Figure 8-1).

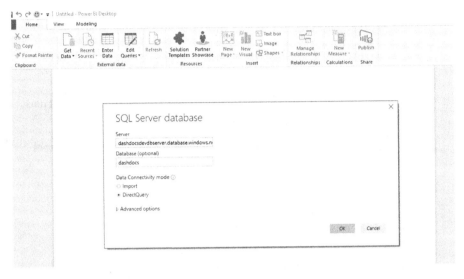

Figure 8-1. *Connecting to the SQL database*

Under the Data connectivity mode, select Direct Query. Direct Query will persist the connection information in the report and connect to the data source and retrieve the data every time we run the report. The import option is suitable when the data changes are infrequent and fine for having scheduled data retrieval.

Click 'Ok' and this will open the next window, where you will enter the database credentials (Figure 8-2). Select Database as the option as we will connect the Azure SQL Database and enter the credentials.

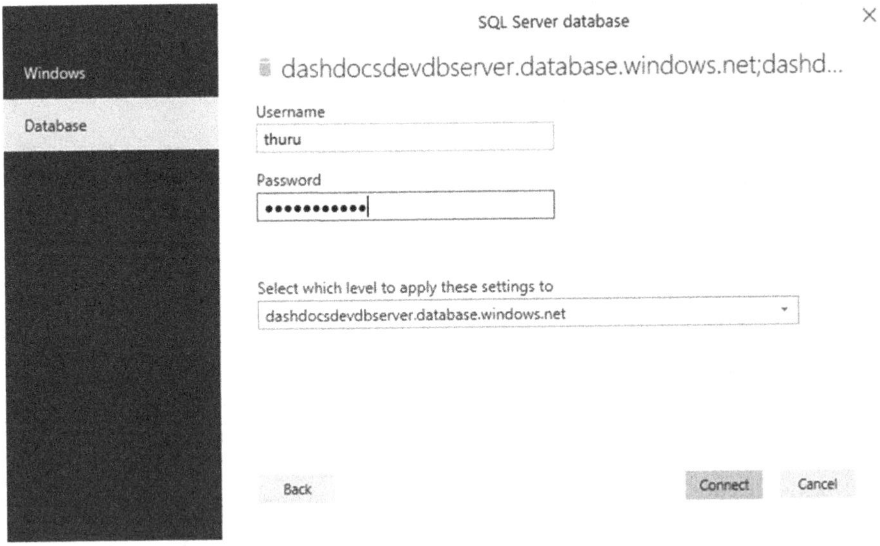

Figure 8-2. *Enter database credentials*

Click 'Connect'; this will connect to the database and retrieves the list of tables in the database; choose the Documents table and DocumentDownloads table for this report (Figure 8-3).

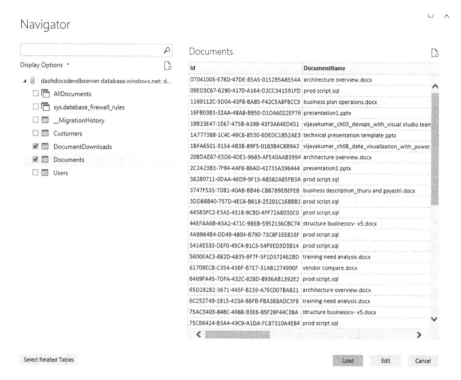

Figure 8-3. *Select required tables*

Then click 'Load' and this will load the data in the Power BI Desktop workspace to start creating the report.

■ **Note**   Power BI Desktop is a rich tool to create Power BI reports, and it supports various data sources and numerous data cleansing and formatting operations. This chapter provides a very straightforward approach to the tool. Read more about the Power BI Desktop tool from this link: https://powerbi.microsoft.com/en-us/documentation/powerbi-desktop-getting-started/

Now drag drop different data visualizations in Power BI to the report workspace and generate a report.

Figure 8-4 shows the report that has the download count against each document name in the bar chat and doughnut chart. The grid also has the same information. The line chart shows a time series graph with the standard pattern line for the number of downloads.

Figure 8-4. *Power BI report in the Power BI Desktop designer*

Power BI has the ability to detect the relationships in the data and link them automatically; for example, in the above scenario we use the count of the Id column of the DocumentDownlods table, which gives the number of downloads as each download has a separate row. This has been joined with the DocumentName column of the Documents table using the relationship between the DocumentId column in the DocumentDownloads and the Id column of the Documents table.

Create a report as explained above or a similar one, and save it in the local file system; Power BI files have the pbix extension.

Publish Power BI Files to Azure Power BI Embedded

In order to get started with the Power BI Embedded service we should provision one service instance in Azure. Power BI Embedded is structured as workspace collection, where **one workspace collection has many workspaces and workspaces can have many Power BI reports**.

We can create the Power BI Embedded workspace collection via the portal, and use the readily available Power BI Embedded provisioning sample from [] to create the workspace and publish the report.

Creating Power BI Embedded Service Using the Portal

Navigate to the Azure portal and search for Power BI Embedded (Figure 8-5) and choose the Power BI Embedded service and click 'Create'.

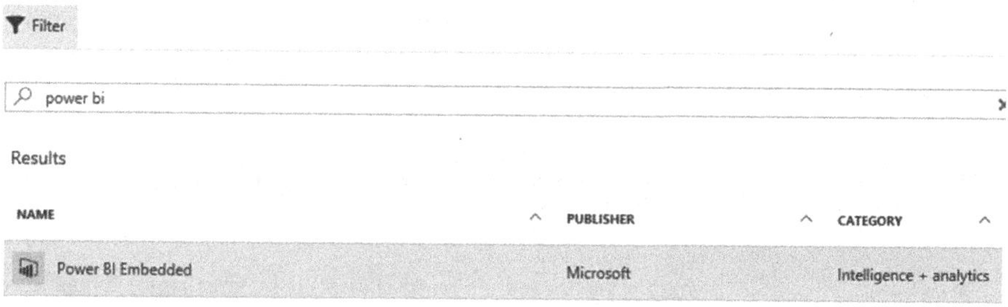

Figure 8-5. *Choosing Power BI Embedded*

This will open Power BI Embedded service creation blade (Figure 8-6). Fill the name of the Power BI Embedded workspace collection and select other usual options including the resource group – DashDocsDev. The pricing tier is locked to standard. **Power BI Embedded is charged for the number of renders in the application. Number of renders are packaged and charged for this service**.

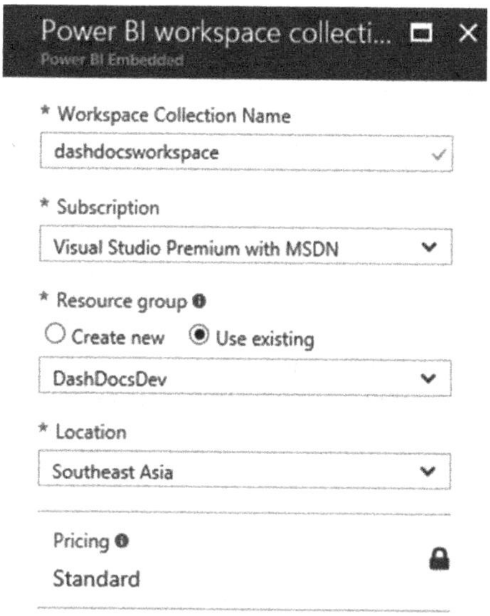

Figure 8-6. *Power BI workspace collection creation blade*

Now we have the Power BI Embedded workspace collection in the resource group; next we should create a workspace and import reports inside the workspace.

Provision the Power BI Embedded Workspace and Publish Reports

In order to manage the Azure Power BI Embedded workspace and publish reports programmatically, we should obtain the Power BI Embedded keys.

Navigate to the Power BI Embedded service in the Azure portal and click the 'Access Keys' section. This will open the access keys blade (Figure 8-7). You can see two access keys; copy one of them and keep it as we will need this.

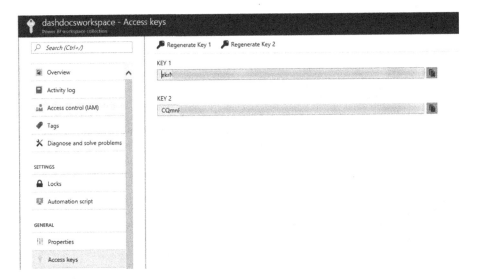

Figure 8-7. *Power BI Embedded access keys*

Now, we have to create the workspace inside the workspace collection and publish the report there. We will use the Power BI Embedded sample application for this purpose. Download the Power BI Embedded sample from this link: `https://github.com/Azure-Samples/power-bi-embedded-integrate-report-into-web-app/`.

Open the solution using Visual Studio, build the solution for the first time, and this will install the missing NuGet packages. Set the startup project to the ProvisioningSample console application.

Open the app.config file of the ProvisioningSample project, and fill the values for the following keys in the app settings.

- subscriptionId – Azure subscription Id

- resourceGroup – Resource group where the Power BI Embedded service is provisioned (DashDocsDev)

- workspaceCollectionName – Name of the workspace collection (dashdocsworkspace)

- accessKey – Use the access key obtained from the portal

The code below snippet shows the app settings section of the app.config.

```
<appSettings file="Cloud.config">
        <!-- Your Azure subscription ID -->
        <add key="subscriptionId" value="" />
        <!-- The Azure resource group name -->
        <add key="resourceGroup" value="" />
        <!-- The Power BI Workspace Collection Name -->
        <add key="workspaceCollectionName" value="" />
        <!-- The Power BI Workspace Collection Access Key -->
        <add key="accessKey" value="" />
        <!-- The Power BI Workspace-->
        <add key="workspaceId" value="" />
        <!-- Credentials to connect to datasource within Power BI -->
        <add key="username" value="" />
        <add key="password" value="" />
    </appSettings>
```

Leave the other settings blank as we would not require them at this point. Run the console application. You will see the first screen of the application (Figure 8-8).

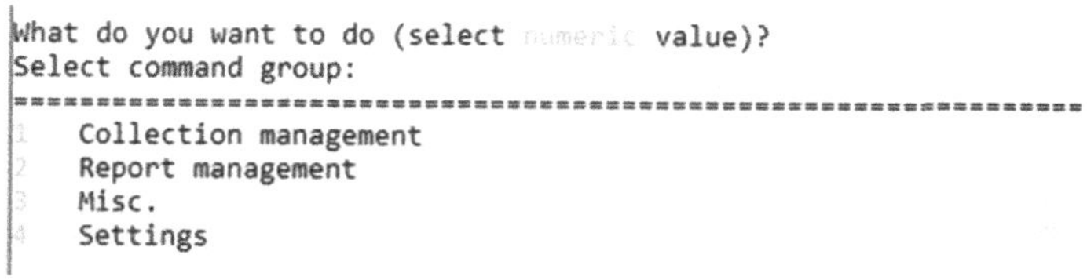

```
What do you want to do (select numeric value)?
Select command group:
=================================================================
    Collection management
    Report management
    Misc.
    Settings
```

Figure 8-8. *Provisioning app main menu*

Choose option 1 – Collection management and hit enter; this will open the collection management menu options (Figure 8-9).

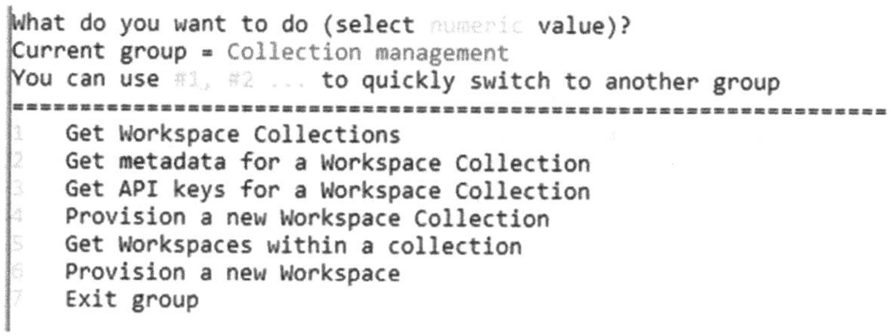

```
What do you want to do (select numeric value)?
Current group = Collection management
You can use #1, #2 ... to quickly switch to another group
=================================================================
    Get Workspace Collections
    Get metadata for a Workspace Collection
    Get API keys for a Workspace Collection
    Provision a new Workspace Collection
    Get Workspaces within a collection
    Provision a new Workspace
    Exit group
```

Figure 8-9. *Collection management menu*

Choose option 6 – Provision a new workspace, as we need to create a new workspace within the existing workspace collection.

This will ask for the workspace collection name; inside is where we want to create the workspace. Since we have provided the workspace collection name in the app settings, the given name will be the default one so we can hit enter to bypass this step.

Next the console will prompt for the workspace name, so enter a name and press enter. The console application will create the workspace and display the workspace Id (Figure 8-10).

```
Workspace Collection Name = dashdocsworkspace. Press enter to use, or give new value:
Workspace Name is required. Enter value:financialreports
```

Figure 8-10. *Creating a workspace inside the workspace collection*

You can create more than one workspace inside a workspace collection. Navigate to the Power BI Embedded service in the Azure portal, and in the overview section you can see the created workspaces with the respective Ids (Figure 8-11).

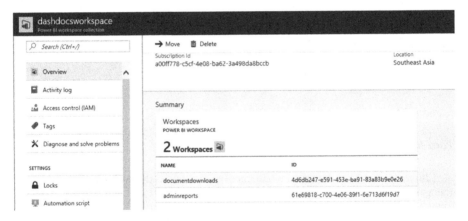

Figure 8-11. *Power BI Embedded workspaces*

Copy the workspace Id inside that we will publish the report, and set the Id in the app settings section of the provisioning sample to make it default.

Run the provisioning sample application again, but this time choose option 2 – Report management from the first menu (Figure 8-8). This will display the report management menu on the screen (Figure 8-12).

```
What do you want to do (select numeric value)?
Current group = Report management
You can use #1, #2 ... to quickly switch to another group
=====================================================================
1    Get Datasets in a workspace
2    Get Reports in a workspace
3    Import PBIX Desktop file into a workspace
4    Get status of PBIX import
5    Delete an imported Dataset
6    Update the Connection String (Cloud only)
7    Update the Connection Credentials (Cloud only)
8    Generate embed details
9    Clone report
10   Rebind report to another dataset
11   Delete report
12   Exit group
```

Figure 8-12. *Report management menu*

Choose option 3 – Import PBIX Desktop file into a workspace; the console will prompt you to enter the workspace collection name, with the default workspace collection name fetched from the app settings.

Then the console will prompt you to enter the workspace Id, with the default workspace Id fetched from the app settings. Next, the console will prompt for the name of the dataset, so enter a name for the dataset. Finally, we should enter the path of the PBIX file we created. This will import the PBIX file to the workspace in Azure (Figure 8-13).

```
Workspace Collection Name = dashdocsworkspace. Press enter to use, or give new value:
Workspace Id = 4d6db247-                        Press enter to use, or give new value:
Dataset Name is required. Enter value:DownloadReport
File Path is required. Enter value:C:\Users\vth\Desktop\document_downloads.pbix
Checking import state... Succeeded
```

Figure 8-13. *Import PBIX desktop file to the workspace*

Copy the dataset Id, since we need this to embed the Power BI report in the web application.

When we import the report, the connection settings (data source connection credentials) of the PBIX file will be removed. We should set the connection string credentials. We can perform this operation using the ProvisioningSample console application.

Launch the application and go to Report management, in the report management menu select option 7 – Update the Connection Credentials (Cloud only). Console will prompt for a series of inputs with the defaults (Figure 8-14). Enter the correct workspace Id and the dataset Id if required.

```
Workspace Collection Name = dashdocsworkspace. Press enter to use, or give new value:
Workspace Id = 4d6db247-                        . Press enter to use, or give new value:
Dataset Id = a9bffbd4-                    . Re-Enter same, or new value:
Username is required. Enter value:thuru
Password is required. Enter value:***********
```

Figure 8-14. *Update the PBIX connection credentials*

Last options will prompt for the username and the password of the connection credentials. This is important to be updated, as our report uses direct query.

Now, we have finished the required steps in publishing the Power BI report to the Azure Power BI Embedded service and updated it with the connection credentials.

Embed Power BI Reports in the Web Application

We have the Power BI report in the Azure Power BI Embedded workspace, and we should embed this report inside the DashDocs web application.

Power BI Embedded service provides an embed token for each report. **Embed token is generated for the unique combination of workspace collection, workspace Id, and report Id.** This embed token will be used in the rendering purpose via the PowerBI JavaScript file.

First let's install the required NuGet packages to perform the embedding actions.

```
Install-Package Microsoft.PowerBI.Api

Install-Package Microsoft.PowerBI.Core
Install-Package Microsoft.PowerBI.AspNet.Mvc
Install-Package Microsoft.PowerBI.JavaScript
```

The Microsoft.PowerBI.Api and Microsoft.PowerBI.Core libraries are required to authenticate to the Azure Power BI Embedded service and acquire the embed token for the report. Microsoft.PowerBI.AspNet.Mvc and Micrsofoft.PowerBI.JavaScript libraries are required in the client side rendering of the Power BI report.

Now, we have all the required NuGet packages in the project. Let's add the required settings parameters for the Power BI Embedded. Add the following information in the app settings of the web.config.

```
<add key="PowerBI:ApiUrl" value="https://api.powerbi.com" />
<add key="PowerBI:WorkspaceCollection" value="<WORKSPACE COLLECTION NAME>" />
<add key="PowerBI:Workspace" value="<WORKSPACE ID>" />
<add key="PowerBI:AccessKey" value="<ACCESS KEY>" />
<add key="PowerBI:ReportId" value="<REPORT ID> " />
```

Let's begin the development by adding a class named PowerBIService in the Services folder. This class will obtain the report parameters and the embed token from the Azure Power BI Embedded service. **Power BI access key is used to authenticate to the Power BI Embedded service.**

PowerBIService.cs

```
public class PowerBIService
    {
        private IPowerBIClient _powerBiClient;
        private string _accessKey;

        public PowerBIService()
        {
            _accessKey = ConfigurationManager.AppSettings["PowerBI:
            AccessKey"].ToString();
            var powerBiUrl = ConfigurationManager.
            AppSettings["PowerBI:ApiUrl"].ToString();

            var credentials = new TokenCredentials(_accessKey, "AppKey");

            _powerBiClient = new PowerBIClient(credentials);
            _powerBiClient.BaseUri = new Uri(powerBiUrl);
        }

        public async Task<ReportViewModel> GetDocumentDownloadReportAsync()
        {
            var workspaceCollection = ConfigurationManager.AppSettings
            ["PowerBI:WorkspaceCollection"].ToString();
            var workspaceId = ConfigurationManager.AppSettings["PowerBI:
            Workspace"].ToString();
            var reportId = ConfigurationManager.
            AppSettings["PowerBI:ReportId"].ToString();

            var reportsResponse = await _powerBiClient.Reports.
            GetReportsAsync(workspaceCollection, workspaceId);
            var report = reportsResponse.Value.FirstOrDefault(r => r.Id ==
            reportId);
            var embedToken = PowerBIToken.CreateReportEmbedToken
            (workspaceCollection, workspaceId, reportId);

            var viewModel = new ReportViewModel
            {
                Report = report,
                AccessToken = embedToken.Generate(_accessKey)
            };

            return viewModel;
        }

    }
```

In the constructor we create the Power BI Client using the access keys obtained from the portal. **Power BI Client object acts as the proxy for the Azure Power BI Embedded REST service.** This proxy is used in the method to obtain the embed token for the report.

GetDocumentDownloadAsync method returns a view model object (ReportViewModel, which has two properties, Report and the AccessToken. This view model is passed to the MVC View and rendered in HTML.

ReportViewModel.cs

```
public class ReportViewModel
    {
        public Report Report { get; set; }
        public string AccessToken { get; set; }
    }
```

Let's add a new MVC controller to handle the report requests and respond with the ReportViewModel object. Add a controller named PowerBIController in the Controllers folder.

PowerBIController.cs

```
[Authorize]
    public class PowerBIController : Controller
    {
        public async Task<ActionResult> Index()
        {
            var poweBIService = new PowerBIService();
            var viewModel = await poweBIService.
            GetDocumentDownloadReportAsync();

            return View(viewModel);
        }
    }
```

Add an empty View for the Index action. This view will have the HTML and JavaScript code for the report embedding.

Views/PowerBI/Index.cshtml

```
@model DashDocs.ViewModels.ReportViewModel

@{
    ViewBag.Title = "Report";
}

<script src="~/Scripts/jquery-3.1.1.min.js"></script>
<script src="~/Scripts/powerbi.min.js"></script>

<div class="col-md-12 bg-blue">
    <h2>@Model.Report.Name</h2>
</div>
```

```
<div class="col-md-12 page-content">
    @Html.PowerBIReportFor(m => m.Report, new { id = "pbi-report", style =
    "height:85vh", powerbi_access_token = Model.AccessToken })
</div>

<script>
    $(function () {
        var reportElement = document.getElementById('pbi-report');

        var report = powerbi.embed(reportElement);
    });
</script>
```

@Html.PowerBIReportFor generates the div with the access token and embed URL. Also, this view has the references to the jQuery and PowerBI JavaScript libraries, which are used in the script.

This script is an IIFE (Immediately Invoked Function Expressions), which looks for the div with the id 'pbi-report' and passes the div element to the Power BI embed method in the Power BI JavaScript library.

▓ **Note**   Power BI JavaScript client library is a feature client SDK for the Power BI Embedded. We can apply filters, navigations, and events to the Power BI report. You can read more about that from this link: https://github.com/Microsoft/PowerBI-JavaScript

---

Now, we have completed the embedding of our report. When you run the application you will see the embedded report inside the DashDocs application (Figure 8-15).

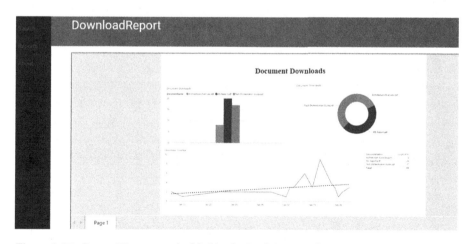

Figure 8-15. *Power BI report embedded in the DashDocs application*

Summary

In this chapter, we provisioned the Power BI Embedded service in Azure, created a Power BI report using the Power BI Desktop, published the report, and embedded the report in our application.

You can download the source code of this chapter from this `https://github.com/thuru/DashDocs/tree/master/DashDocs/Chapter%208`.

Figure 8-16 shows the overview of the DashDocs application.

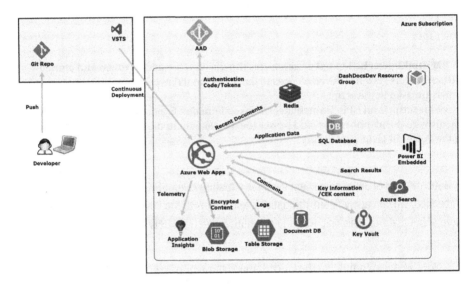

Figure 8-16. *DashDocs application overview*

Index

© Thurupathan Vijayakumar 2017
T. Vijayakumar, *Practical Azure Application Development*, DOI 10.1007/978-1-4842-2817-3

■ V

■ W, X, Y, Z

Get the eBook for only $5!

Why limit yourself?

With most of our titles available in both PDF and ePUB format, you can access your content wherever and however you wish—on your PC, phone, tablet, or reader.

Since you've purchased this print book, we are happy to offer you the eBook for just $5.

To learn more, go to http://www.apress.com/companion or contact support@apress.com.

Apress®

Printed in the United States
By Bookmasters